BECOMING A
JUSTICE
SEEKING
CONGREGATION

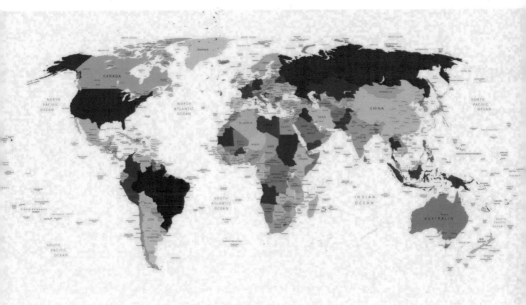

Responding to God's Justice Initiative

WILLIAM K. MCELVANEY

Becoming a Justice Seeking Congregation

Responding to God's Justice Initiative

William K. McElvaney

Foreword by Tex Sample

iUniverse, Inc.
New York   Bloomington

Becoming a Justice Seeking Congregation
Responding to God's Justice Initiative

iUniverse books may be ordered through booksellers or by contacting:

iUniverse
1663 Liberty Drive
Bloomington, IN 47403
www.iuniverse.com
1-800-Authors (1-800-288-4677)

Because of the dynamic nature of the Internet, any Web addresses or links contained in this book may have changed since publication and may no longer be valid.

ISBN: 978-1-4401-5353-2 (sc)
ISBN: 978-1-4401-5355-6 (dj)
ISBN: 978-1-4401-5354-9 (ebk)

Printed in the United States of America

iUniverse rev. date: 8/24/2009

OTHER BOOKS BY WILLIAM K. MCELVANEY

Christ's Suburban Body (Abingdon Press, 1970)
Co-authored with Wilfred M. Bailey

The Saving Possibility (Abingdon Press, 1971)

Cerebrations on Coming Alive (Abingdon Press, 1973)

Good News is Bad News is Good News (Orbis Books, 1980)
Chinese edition, Chinese Christian Literature Council Ltd.,
1988

The People of God in Ministry (Abingdon Press, 1981)

Preaching from Camelot to Covenant (Abingdon Press, 1989)

Winds of Grace, Ways of Faith (Westminster/John Knox Press, 1991)

Eating and Drinking at the Welcome Table (Chalice Press, 1998)

CONTENTS

ACKNOWLEDGMENTS

This book could not possibly have come to fruition without the indispensable assistance of Frances Owens McElvaney, my adult lifetime lover, best friend, and director of the McElvaney Computer Department. In my own eyes I have never quite fit the description of being a Luddite, though occasionally accused of such by nerdy computer friends. After all, I did manage to put the manuscript on the computer. English major Fran made all the corrections, managed the files, formatted the manuscript for electronic submittal, and handled most of the back and forth communication with iUniverse. My first solo authored book, *The Saving Possibility* (1971) was dedicated to Fran. What goes around comes around. *Becoming a Justice Seeking Congregation* follows suit. This second dedication is not only for Fran's manuscript empowerment but also for her own justice commitment that has been instructive for me.

I am extremely grateful to our daughter Shannon who has taught Fran and me more than I can say about environmental protection and justice. Our son John's prejudice-free work ethic in conservative East Texas exemplifies much of the spirit of this book.

I have always considered myself to be a slow learner. Slow learners need many mentors. Through the years I have been richly blessed with a sizable diversity of insightful and generous friends and colleagues who have been my teachers and guides. By the time one reaches 80 plus, there are more people to thank than can be remembered!

Acknowledgments in previous books have expressed gratitude to my parents, pastors, and to Perkins School of Theology professors who have shaped my faith from youth through seminary days into early adulthood. The gracious people of First Methodist Church in Justin, Texas, taught a city boy just out of seminary how to be and do ministry in a rural setting. My appreciation remains for a lifetime. I will always be grateful to the people of St. Stephen and Northaven United Methodist Churches for courage to take justice risks and for encouragement of my attempts to lead in that direction. I am indebted to the bold justice witness and collegial leadership of the Saint Paul School of Theology faculty during my twelve years as president of the seminary.

Many friends, both clerical and lay, have been my teachers and co-workers over the years as we have reflected and worked together for justice in a variety of causes and settings. Persons listed here represent many others not named who are also committed to justice, yet with whom I have had less opportunity to be about the ongoing task of justice.

Film credits at the end of movies often provide acknowledgments to film crews in more than one location. Thus, heartfelt thanks to the Dallas Area justice crew for years of faithful justice vocation: Gail and Jim Smith, George and Jeannette Crawford, Jan Sanders, Ron Wilhelm and Kim Batchelor, Ken and Joanna Shields, Carole Carsey, Marilaine Jones, Harry and Betty Thompson, Shirley Cooper, Adriana Cobo-Frenkel, Don and Judy Lambert, Lew King, Bob Cooper, Ray Flachmeier, Joyce and Mac Hall, Rita Clarke, Nancy Boye, Liz Branch, Wil Finnin, Jerry Longwell, Peter Johnson, Charles Stovall, Zan Holmes, Bill and Norma Matthews, Rob Evans, Mark Herbener, Mary Mitchell Trimble, and Evans Mank.

The Kansas City Area justice unit members are Gene and Sarah Lowry, Paul Jones, Fran and Tom Manson, and Marie Whitmer. They have provided rich pastoral and prophetic examples to ponder and emulate.

Vicky Stifter and John Boonstra, Susan Edenborough, Dick Raines, and Bill Steel represent a widespread West Coast crew for whom I am immensely grateful.

The almost weekly presence in our lives of John and Ann Davis and Lisa Holmes and Mary Mallory make them special sustainers of all that Fran and I take on. George Purvis is an inspirational crew of one whose theological vision transcends his deeply troubled eyesight.

The eleven writers in Chapter 5, each in his or her own way, have contributed to my awareness of justice strategies. Much appreciation goes to Eric Folkerth, my former seminary student and presently my pastor, for commitment to justice and for generosity of spirit.

The blessed memory of Rabbi Levi Olan, Jerry Hobbs, Bourdon Smith, Wilfred Bailey, Charles Baughman, Andrew Weaver, Paul Whitmer, and Parker and Jean Wilson continues to bless my life. The same is true for remembrance of many "saints" of the First United Methodist Church in Elma, Washington; the First United Methodist Church, Justin, Texas; St. Stephen and Northaven congregations; and Saint Paul and Perkins Schools of Theology.

I extend special appreciation to Walter Brueggemann, Zan Holmes, Tex Sample, and Jeannie Trevino-Teddlie for reading the manuscript and offering both support and timely suggestions for consideration. The final result is better for their having given time and thought, yet of course the limitations of the work belong to me alone. George Baldwin provided valuable assistance in details of manuscript preparation and submittal.

I am grateful to Susanne Johnson, Valerie Karras, and Jeannie Trevino-Teddlie of the Perkins School of Theology faculty for our shared efforts of public resistance to the President George W. Bush Policy Institute at Southern Methodist University.

A number of organizations and groups have provided gifts of insight, inspiration, and humor so necessary for staying the course in justice seeking and doing. These life-giving entities include the Church in Society (CIS) Commission of Northaven United Methodist Church; the Dallas Peace Center; the Reconciling Ministries Network; The Cathedral of Hope; Maria Madre de los Pobres Roman Catholic parish in San Salvador; Midway Hills Christian Church; a motley crew of clergy colleagues known as the Dirty Dozen; a group of retired Saint Paul School of Theology faculty self-named as Camelot; and last but far from least, a remnant of St. Stephenites known as the Bridge Group.

All of these acknowledgments take their rightful place within the larger framework of gratitude above all for God's amazing grace freely given.

FOREWORD

Bill McElvaney has spent a lifetime working for justice and peace, locally, nationally, and internationally. As a courageous pastor, a prophetic seminary president, and a socially engaged professor, the ethical mission of the church was and is central to his life and work.

This book represents the fruit of his thought and action. Further, it reflects his collegial style with the addition of brief, illuminating articles by his friends and colleagues in justice and peace ministries. Here are concrete ideas for working in social ministry; here is challenge; here are specific steps for us to pursue, indeed, to live. I heartily recommend this book.

… Tex Sample, Robert B. and Kathleen Rogers Professor Emeritus of Church and Society, Saint Paul School of Theology, Kansas City, Missouri

Author's proceeds from the sale of this book will support Organization for Development of the Indigenous Maya (ODIM), Guatemala, and the Dallas Peace Center.

INTRODUCTION

Like most books *Becoming a Justice Seeking Congregation* has been in the making for a period of years. During the actual writing time of several months, and long before, I have been acutely aware of the dilemma of many pastors and congregations: concern about declining membership, financial stability, building upkeep, and an uncertain future. These concerns are presently more pronounced due to the existing national and global economic crisis.

During my fifteen years as a pastor in both rural and suburban congregations I often struggled between being weighed down by institutional realities and being lifted up by covenant freedom and courage. At times I found it easy to dismiss the message of the prophets and to select the parts of Jesus' life and ministry compatible with personal and institutional comfort. The prophets of social justice didn't have to worry about losing synagogue members who financed a religious institution. They didn't have buildings to maintain, reports to turn in to ecclesiastical authorities, or families to support with salaries provided by others.

With all of the above in mind, a book encouraging congregations to embrace the difficult vocation of justice may seem to be a voice crying in the wilderness. Whether a congregation takes on justice ministry depends, in part, on its concept of God and God's purpose for the Church and for life itself. I say in part because engaging justice also depends on discerning how popular church culture works against justice orientation, the willingness to ask new justice-based questions, and the courage to initiate a new direction. Chapters 4 and 5 offer some possibilities.

According to the Hebrew prophets God's covenant with Israel makes social justice an imperative reflecting the very character of

God. For Christians Jesus exemplifies the prophetic tradition and is the personification and embodiment of God's love and justice. Since Jesus' ministry is our ministry as Christians, the church is called to be a sacrament of God's purpose in the world. Justice, an expression of God's love, is not optional for those who would follow faithfully in the footsteps of Jesus.

Becoming a Justice Seeking Congregation is an invitation and challenge to wrestle with the Church's God-given vocation of justice. I'm convinced that if a congregation deprives itself of biblically based justice vocation, it downsizes the life, death, and resurrection of Jesus. Not only that, the liberating discovery God makes possible for justice seeking Christians is cut off.

If you in this country keep working in whatever ways you can for the crucified peoples of the earth – in the United States, in El Salvador, wherever – your lives will have more meaning; your faith will be more Christian; your hope will be stronger.
        … Jon Sobrino, S.J., El Salvador[1]

Where Does This Book Come From?

Much of the book's content was shaped from my own trial and error ministry of discernment and discovery in seeking and doing justice. Fifteen years in the pastorate honed my sense of defining and taking on justice issues. A total of twenty years as a seminary president and professor in two United Methodist seminaries afforded a learning curve with students as we explored Christian justice vocation and practice. My focus in these settings became increasingly centered on peace and justice issues informed by biblical, theological, and liturgical grounding as well as the example of others to whom I am greatly indebted. My mentors have included African-American, Latino/a, feminist, third world, Native American, GLBT writers, lecturers, and friends. I have also learned from persons with disabilities. My journey in coming to grips with the call of justice is narrated in Chapter 4.

Why This Book?

In my reading and in my conversation with pastors and seminary students I became convinced of a sizable need for hands on, rubber hits the road, local church kind of justice treatment. I have been impressed with both written and electronic offerings of sound scholarship related to the prophets and Jesus. I'm indebted, too, to works providing keen analysis of the condition of our world and our nation. These features will not be absent in this book (Chapters 1 and 2), but they will not characterize my main intent or content.

Chapter 3 lifts up God's gifts for strengthening our commitment to justice, serving as a bridge from Chapters 1 and 2 to Chapters 4 and 5.

What I'm after and what I believe will serve congregations well is specific treatment of the idealism and realism of our justice vocation; reflection on nonviolent strategies available for clergy and laity to consider; specific instances of justice seeking and doing in my own ministry (Chapter 4); examples of justice action from a variety of local churches and other sources (Chapter 5). Basically this book is a strategic manual addressing not only the why, what, and where questions but, above all, the how questions related to doing justice by local congregations and by seminary students. My church tradition, Wesleyan and United Methodist, states our purpose as that of making disciples of Jesus Christ for the transformation of the world. This endeavor is rightly grounded in changing hearts and minds of individuals for Christian discipleship. Yet if we are to be realists, following Jesus cannot end there. The world will not experience transformation without a vocation of justice addressing systemic injustices on behalf of the common good.

Suggestions for Reading the Book

This book is intended for clergy, laity, and seminary students. The orientation is ecumenical and interfaith with particular familiarity and indebtedness to my own United Methodist tradition.

I recommend group study whether in church school classes, leadership groups, mission/outreach committees, or task groups who have a passion for justice yet need some insight and inspiration on how to get started and take on a selected justice issue. The book can also serve as study material for clergy groups and seminary classes who want to move beyond theory into the practice of prophetic ministry. The questions at the end of each chapter facilitate inquiry, discussion, and making decisions. Some readers will prefer to read on their own or to share with a selected colleague.

For readers experienced and long committed to justice vocation, the book can serve as a teaching resource. For readers willing to take on a fresh invitation and challenge of justice seeking, the book can be a basic learning resource.

My Hope for the Reader

1. To realize anew that justice is deep in the heart and purpose of God.
2. To experience God at a deeper level through justice involvement as did many biblical characters and Christians who have gone before us.
3. To be re-introduced to at least a few glimpses of the prophets and how they speak truth to the church and society today.
4. To see more clearly the justice ministry of Jesus to which the church is called as demonstrated by numerous biblical texts.
5. To gain strength and courage for taking on justice and clearer insight for justice strategizing and implementation today.
6. To become more convinced than ever that justice is absolutely necessary for the world to have a viable future.

Appendices

In the Appendices the reader will find brief treatments of two issues important for considering justice in a broader context: An Inevitable Connection: Peace and Justice (Appendix A) and A Less Recognized Connection: Pastoral and Prophetic Ministry (Appendix B). The reader may wish to read these reflections prior to reading the book.

Author's Note: My use of language seeks to be inclusive at all levels; however, biblical quotations from the New Revised Standard Version and other sources are left as in the original. Unless otherwise noted, biblical quotations are from the NRSV.

Notes

[1]Fr. Jon Sobrino, colleague of the six Jesuits murdered Nov. 16, 1989, at the University of Central America, San Salvador. These words were spoken at an interfaith prayer service in San Francisco, Dec. 1, 1989.

SECTION I

FOUNDATIONS OF JUSTICE

CHAPTER 1

THE SOURCE OF JUSTICE

*For the Lord of hosts has a day against all that is proud
and lofty, against all that is lifted up and high.*

Isaiah 2:12

*I have put my spirit upon him; he will bring forth justice
to the nations.*

Isaiah 42:1

Where does the idea of justice come from and who says so? Must one
have roots in a religious tradition to have or develop a heart and mind
of justice?

Can you retrace your sense of justice, however defined, to its roots
earlier in your life to the present? As I write I'm returning momentarily
to my childhood and early adolescent years. I invite you to do the same
as you read and reflect. Early on I had a sense of concern for kids who
seemed weak or at a physical disadvantage. This awareness may have
come from being a sickly child with asthma so wretched that I started
to public school a year late. I was already developing an incipient
"underdog theology" to be recognized as such many years later. In
addition I absorbed some sense of fairness and concern for others from
my parents and The Methodist Church. Even so my awareness was very
limited and selective. What does your story look like?

As will be indicated in Chapter 4, social justice became a clearer
concept and claim on my life as a seminary student. Studying the
Hebrew prophets of social justice and the Reign of God proclaimed

and embodied through Jesus brought a profound change. Yet it was the actual social reality of injustice encountered in and around my parish as a young pastor that tested my theological education and my capacity to respond.

I believe many persons, depending in part on the variables and instilled values of their upbringing, realize a sense of fairness and equity apart from specific religious attachment or commitment. Have we not all known others who say they are not "religious," yet have a keener sense of justice than many who claim to be persons of faith? And is it not so that most of us, whether we claim to be religious or not, may develop a feeling or understanding of justice and equality in some areas while lacking in others? The same person can vary greatly in attitudes about race, gender, class, and sexual orientation. An individual can be enlightened in one of these areas while biased, fearful, or even hostile in another.

Some Christians may be offended that persons who claim no religious faith can be more justice oriented than some of us church folk. To the contrary I take great comfort in the realization that God is loose in the world, not confined to institutional labels or boundaries. The Holy Spirit blows at will.

Some Christian theologians refer to this creation given availability of moral awareness as natural law or simply a theology of creation. The Roman Catholic belief in natural law is well documented in the Catechism of the Catholic Church. The natural law is understood to be present in the heart of each person as the gift of the Creator. The wisdom tradition in scripture often appeals to human reason seemingly beyond revealed commandments of God. Whatever we choose to call it, and however arrived at, we can be grateful for justice allies within and beyond the church.

Whether our view of justice as Christians is shaped by God's gift of reason (natural law given in creation) or through Jesus and the prophets of social justice (revealed theology of grace and response), or both, there is widespread agreement among Christians that God is the source of justice.

A Primary Source of the Source

Biblical scholars have made a clear case that we see Jesus or "get" to Jesus through the witness and writings of the early church, and even so with a great variety of images. The same is true of our access to the Hebrew prophets and the Torah from which we as Christians learn deep truths about justice. The written word, with all of its fallibility and misuses through the years, is still our umbilical cord to the source of life and justice represented by Jesus and the prophets. Some of us might refer to scripture as "a source of the source" in developing our sense of justice.

At the same time, depending on our particular faith tradition, Christians also use a combination of sources in identifying the various kinds and claims of justice. My United Methodist brothers and sisters employ scripture, tradition, reason, and experience to round out our theological understanding of our justice vocation. Most Christian bodies rely on some combination of these factors for faith and action with different emphasis or weight assigned to each. How would you grapple with these sources of authority in your faith community, especially related to justice?

Insights from Hebrew Scripture

In his classic *Theology of the Old Testament*, Walter Brueggemann states Israel's claim:

"From the outset, Yahweh is known to be a God committed to the establishment of concrete, sociopolitical justice in a world of massive power organized against justice." He goes on to say:

"Israel, everywhere and without exhaustion, is preoccupied with the agenda of justice that is rooted in the character and resolve of Yahweh." [1]

In his book *Let Justice Roll Down*, Bruce C. Birch provides similar insights into the source of justice: "Covenant faithfulness required of Israel the effort to embody justice, righteousness, and steadfast love in systemic social structures and practices."[2]

"These qualities (justice and righteousness) are rooted in the character of God who has acted in justice and righteousness toward the people. God then expects these qualities to be reflected in the life of God's people in their relationships to one another and to God."[3]

"Justice is a chief attribute of God's activity in the world ... the *Mishpat* of God is experienced by the vulnerable in the community as 'justice,' the upholding of their rights and the advocacy of their need ... God's justice and righteousness is especially manifest in care for the poor, the hungry, the widow, the orphan, the oppressed, the troubled, the afflicted."[4]

A Consideration of Hebrew Words and Texts

It is not the intention of this book or this chapter to offer an in-depth analysis of Hebrew words used for justice and righteousness. Even a cursory examination reveals several meanings of key words depending on the context in which each word is used. What can be said accurately and briefly is this: the Hebrew word most frequently used for justice is *mishpa*t, as interpreted in the quotes from Birch's *Let Justice Roll Down*. Perhaps the best known use of *mishpat* is in Amos, "Let justice roll down like waters ... " (5:24). In Micah's oft quoted "to do justice ..." (6:8), again *mishpat* is used.

A key word for God's righteousness is *sedeq*, masculine, and *sedequah*, feminine. Like *mishpat* these words have a number of interpretations. "When applied to God, righteousness implies the covenant relationship which God has initiated with Israel."[5]

"The first thing to underline about these two words is their theocentric foundation. The righteous and just God who commands his people to imitate his justice is the source and foundation of human justice."[6]

These Hebrew words remind us of the long historical attempt by faith predecessors to name and to do justice. The larger context in which they appeared was usually fraught with struggle, risk, and frequent failure as prophets called to proclaim "the word of the Lord." We neglect them at the peril of our ministry, our churches, our nation. We do well to sit at their feet as seekers of wisdom and courage, as inquirers of the profound and the enduring.

Throughout this book biblical texts will be gently sprinkled into chosen locations as witnesses on behalf of justice. Sometimes they raise provocative questions. At other times they provide moral guidance or even imperatives. As we reflect on God as the source of justice and life, take a few moments to meditate on these passages from the Psalms and the Prophets:

"He loves righteousness and justice; the earth is full of the steadfast love of the Lord." (Ps. 33:5)

"For the Lord loves justice; he will not forsake his faithful ones." (Ps. 37:28)

"Give justice to the weak and the orphan; maintain the right of the lowly and the destitute. Rescue the weak and the needy; deliver them from the hand of the wicked." (From Ps. 82 in which God makes a plea for justice in the divine council)

"Righteousness and justice are the foundations of his throne." (Ps. 97:2)

"Justice is turned back, and righteousness stands at a distance; for truth stumbles in the public square, and uprightness cannot enter." (Is. 59:14)

"With what shall I come before the Lord, and bow myself before God on high? He has told you, O mortal, what is good: and what does the Lord require of you but to do justice, and to love kindness, and to walk humbly with your God." (from Micah 6:6-8)

These texts serve as witnesses and pointers to the larger context in which each occurs.

Jesus and Justice

The New Testament is a breeding ground for justice vocation. As Christians we look to Jesus above all as the exemplar of justice. A breaking forth of justice images throughout the New Testament is also discernible in certain Pauline passages, the book of James, and other epistles. Before centering our attention on Jesus and justice, I call attention to Paul's first letter to the Corinthians, especially I Cor. 1:18-31, with focus on vs. 26-29.

Speaking of the mostly low brow Corinthians, and perhaps with the cross of Jesus in mind, Paul gave verse to God's troubling but liberating penchant for surprise and the culturally absurd: "Consider your call, brothers and sisters; not many of you were wise by human standards, not many were powerful, not many were of noble birth. But God chose what is foolish in the world to shame the wise; God chose what is weak in the world to shame the strong; God chose what is low and despised in the world, things that are not, to reduce to nothing the things that are, so that no one might boast in the presence of God." The New English Bible translates vs. 28 as "God has chosen things low and contemptible, mere nothings, to overthrow the existing order." These words of Paul are reminiscent of the Magnificat in Luke 1 revealing God's preferential option for those of low standing in the world. Here Paul and Jesus are on the same theological page whereupon God reverses human wisdom.

Shifting now to the gospels, Luke is especially clear in portraying Jesus the bearer in word and deed of justice as an expression of God's love. After all, the New Testament God of Jesus is the same God of the Torah, the Psalms, and the prophets of social justice in whose tradition Jesus emerges.

Jesus uses the image or paradigm of the Reign of God as the framework of God's justice. In the Nazareth synagogue Jesus proclaimed his mission as a sign of the in-breaking Reign of God: "The Spirit of the Lord is upon me, because he has anointed me to bring good news to the poor. He has sent me to proclaim release to the captives, and recovery of sight to the blind, to let the oppressed go free, to proclaim the year of the Lord's favor." (Luke 4:18-19 with origin in Isaiah 61)

The prophets often spoke in the context of monarchy, addressing issues of injustice to kings and the wealthy of Israel and Judah. Jesus, on the other hand, spoke most directly to an oppressed people under Roman occupation. Justice was not in the hands of Jesus' followers and audiences. He spoke of the Reign of God, an all-encompassing message for a people under occupation, yet with implications for the Jewish establishment and the Roman oppressors. His message at Nazareth set forth the priorities of his ministry, echoing the Jewish prophetic tradition of justice and fulfilling the Lord's jubilee announced in Leviticus.

All the signs of God's New Order are subversive of present unjust social realities wherever they occur. The Reign of God is at once both religious and political. It is religious because it comes from beyond human origin or control. It proclaims economic justice but is more than the ideology of class struggle because it is grounded in God's steadfast love and hope for true community. The Reign of God is theological because it cannot finally be identified solely with a political party or any particular scheme of social enhancement. In short God's Reign brings judgment and liberation beyond human calculation or design.

The Reign of God is profoundly political because it demands justice in both procedural and distributive ways in order to restore true community, thus disturbing existing unjust power arrangements. The Reign of God is political because it speaks to real conditions in the here and now, reflecting the "Thy kingdom come, thy will be done on earth as it is in heaven" of the Lord's Prayer. Good news to the poor is bad news for the rich unless and until the wealthy accept God's rearrangements of existing disparity that dehumanizes the poor. Years ago in my book *Good News is Bad News is Good News* (Orbis Books), I wrote that God loves the marginalized by working through all possible nonviolent means to bring justice. And further, that God loves the oppressor enough to disturb mind and heart into new thinking and acting as advocates for justice in God's name.

Turning from Luke to Matthew's gospel, there are two passages that speak of Jesus as advocate for justice. Chapter 12:15-21 is a derivative of Isaiah 42:1-4 in which God's servant will bring forth justice to the nations, identified as Gentiles in Matthew. This text is addressed in Chapter Three under the sub-title, "The Written Word."

The other Matthew passage referring to justice is 23:23 in which Jesus upbraids scribes and Pharisees for neglecting the weightier matters of the law, namely, justice, mercy, and faith (echoes of Micah's 6:6-8 trilogy). He tells them they should have practiced these without neglecting their tithes. Luke's similar reference to justice is a version of Matthew's. Luke uses a string of woes, one of which is "You tithe mint and rue and herbs of all kinds and neglect justice and the love of God; it is these you ought to have practiced, without neglecting the others." (11:42) Modern day tithers, pay attention!

Justice Present, Yet Unnamed

In W. H. Auden's *For the Time Being (A Christmas Oratorio),* there is a section titled, "The Massacre of the Innocents." I read the Oratorio every year as an Advent discipline of preparation. At one point Herod, in a mood of anxiety and bewilderment, exclaims, "Today apparently judging by the trio who came to see me this morning with an ecstatic grin on their scholarly faces, the job has been done. God has been born, they cried, we have seen him ourselves. The World is saved. Nothing else matters."

Herod goes on to expound, "One needn't be much of a psychologist to realize that if this rumour is not stamped out now, in a few years it is capable of diseasing the whole empire, and one doesn't have to be a prophet to predict the consequences if it should."[7]

Diseasing the whole empire with unthinkable consequences! Justice lurks around the corner in many New Testament images and metaphors but not necessarily named as such. Good News to the poor. Liberation of the oppressed. The first shall be last, the last first. Peacemakers, a.k.a. troublemakers, blessed. Religious and cultural boundaries stretched beyond recognition. Undesirables restored to community. Late employed laborers paid the same as all day workers. The mighty put down from their thrones. The proud scattered and the rich sent away empty. Question raising parables mocking empire. Need more be said? Surely not, but if so, one need not be a New Testament scholar to locate ample scriptural evidence of God's call to justice. Herod got the point without ever hearing the word justice. His time was short. No wonder he was shaking in his sandals.

Similar claims can be made for Paul's insistence that "every knee should bend" and "every tongue confess that Jesus Christ is Lord." (Phil. 2:9-11) The word justice is not used, yet Caesar is dethroned in Paul's message proclaimed throughout the Mediterranean world of the Roman Empire. The new order of God's Reign through Jesus Christ, an order of peace, reconciliation, and justice, is to command allegiance instead of to Caesar's empire built on violence, domination, and injustice. No message could have been more radical at the time.

The Source of Justice: What's at Stake?

When I was a professor of preaching and worship at Perkins School of Theology I asked students to raise a number of questions about their sermons. One of the questions was, "What's at stake in this sermon? What difference do you hope it will make in the lives of your congregation?" The same inquiry applies to the source of justice, "What's at stake here?"

I believe "how we do church" is at stake when we reflect on the source of justice. If we think justice is simply the agenda of liberal folks in the church, it will not commend itself to others as intrinsic to the church's being. If we think justice is primarily an Old Testament matter, it becomes a low priority for most Christians. If we believe the world is in such bad shape that justice seeking and doing can make no difference whatsoever, we give up before we get started. If we convince ourselves that seeking justice is just too risky, we "do church" in a self-protecting manner as though the church exists primarily for itself.

On the other hand, if we embrace the many biblical passages lifting up justice as rooted in God's character, we are more likely to take justice to both heart and mind. As we become more aware that God has a special concern for orphans and widows, we are led to ask different questions on the way we go about being the church. We might experience what justice seeking churches frequently discover. There are thoughtful people hoping and looking for a congregation not in bondage to a smooth talking god who glosses over suffering, a happy-go-lucky god selling cheap prosperity with a preferential option for slick and easy solutions.

My experience as a pastor is that while some may leave as a result of the church taking on justice issues, there are others drawn to a congregation willing to speak out and engage deep and troubling issues of injustice. Courage for peacemaking, radical hospitality, and justice vocation will commend itself to some who have given up on the church. But finally it's not about size of membership, it's about the size of our love issuing forth in pastoral and prophetic ministry.

Can we take the word of the Hebrew prophets that God is the source of justice? The late Rabbi Abraham Heschel liked to say, "There are no proofs for the existence of God; there are only witnesses."

Notes

[1]Walter Brueggemann, *Theology of the Old Testament*, Fortress Press, 1997, p. 736.
[2]Bruce C. Birch, *Let Justice Roll Down*, Westminster/John Knox Press, 1991, p. 178.
[3]Birch, p. 260.
[4]Birch, pp. 155-156.

[5]Birch, p. 154.
[6]Birch, p. 107.
[7]W. H. Auden, *Collected Larger Poems*, Vintage Books, 1975, p. 188.

Questions for Reflection and Discussion

1. What influences from childhood to adulthood have shaped your understanding of justice?

2. What determines whether or not a congregation seeks to do justice?

3. In Matthew 23 Jesus insisted that although financial support of the synagogue was expected, justice was more important. How does your congregation respond to Jesus' priority?

4. In what ways does the Reign of God call for justice?

5. How does your church wrestle with the authority of scripture, tradition, reason, and experience in serving and doing justice?

6. How does your understanding of justice relate to biblical insights from the Hebrew Scripture and the New Testament?

CHAPTER 2

THE SIGNS OF JUSTICE

Justice is the order love requires.

Daniel Day Williams

Justice is the way societies and institutions and governments best love each other.

Lane Denson

The World in Which We Seek Justice

Justice is absolutely necessary for the world to have a viable future. This claim becomes readily apparent in any serious analysis of the world today. Unless we have hibernated in a cave for an extended period of time, we are aware of a world in big trouble in more ways than we can name. The litany includes widespread personal and systemic violence; huge expenditures on weapon development without calling it an arms race; depletion of natural resources which author Richard Heinberg calls "peak everything;" millions living in poverty and lacking health care; millions homeless and displaced; pollution and global warming. This is the world in which we as Christians are called to a vocation of justice.

As one would expect, different authors name the world's accelerating turmoil in various frameworks of image and language. Jim Winkler, General Secretary, General Board of Church and Society, United Methodist Church, has spoken of the powerful and intertwined demonic systems holding the earth in their grip: hunger making, war making, and desert making. He states further, "Our lives are intimately bound up in a moral, spiritual crisis of profound and unprecedented dimensions. The reigning model of economic globalization threatens earth's life systems, undermines cultural integrity and diversity, and endangers the lives of many who are poor in order that some might consume exorbitantly and few accumulate vast wealth." (from GBCS newsletter, *Faith in Action*, June 20, 2008)

In his book *Everything Must Change*, Brian McLaren uses a metaphor "suicide machine" to describe the world's crisis (he gives credit to Leonard Sweet for the term). The suicide machine is fueled by environmental breakdown, the growing disparity between rich and poor, the danger of cataclysmic war, and the failure of the world's religions to provide healing or at least reduction of the primary causes. The suicide machine is an accurate description of the present world crisis. It suggests a global demise we do to ourselves which is surely the case. In naming the world's current condition the term "human sacrifice" also commends itself to me as a key social and global reality. It denotes destruction done <u>to</u> others <u>by</u> those who wield power and privilege.

Human sacrifice is not something practiced only by ancient Aztecs and other Mesoamerica civilizations. Whether ancient or modern, empire seeking, the opposite of justice seeking, requires human sacrifice of its own citizens and of its enemies to feed the appetite of hubris and domination through military, economic, or political means, or usually a combination. To the contrary, think of Frederick Douglass, Sojourner Truth, Rosa Parks, Martin Luther King, Jr., Cesar Chavez, Susan B. Anthony, Elizabeth Cady Stanton, Vine Deloria, Russell Means, Harvey Milk, and a host of others who worked and sacrificed for justice. Their names remind us of the long standing injustices in and by our country, the path of systemic progress to which they contributed, and the remaining unresolved influence of the past on the present.

During the first eight years of the twenty-first century, many of the well documented policies and practices of the George W. Bush administration typified the reaches of empire: a pre-emptive war of choice based on false premises without regard for international opinion; approval of torture and rendition based on a misbegotten belief in

American exceptionalism; violation of human rights domestically and abroad under the label of national security or democracy; the most secret, least transparent U.S. government since the Nixon administration; continuation of the expansion of U.S. military bases in at least 125 countries around the world.

I'm not suggesting that our leaders deliberately sought to sacrifice others to pursue their own interests, or in their minds, the national interest of the United States. I am suggesting the consequences of empire seeking inevitably result in human sacrifice, whether by the United States or any country. One only has to read Stephen Kinzer's *Overthrow, America's Century of Regime Change from Hawaii to Iraq* in order to realize that infatuation with Manifest Destiny is not new to the United States. The sacrifice of more than 58,000 Americans on the altar of an unnecessary war in Vietnam, as well as the deaths of thousands of Vietnamese, remains a testimony to empire's demonic blindness and willingness to sacrifice lives. The so-called Pax Romana was not about the peace of Rome but about control and domination requiring human sacrifice.

The formula of empire, wherever it manifests itself, is clear and simple: the most vulnerable are the most expendable. As detailed in Kinzer's *Overthrow*, our long U.S. history of disrespect and violation of duly constituted yet vulnerable governments in Latin America and elsewhere is ample testimony to the empire formula. This pattern of ravaging the weak has continued in somewhat different form through the so-called free trade that impoverishes low income farmers in Latin America through the North American Free Trade Agreement and the Central American Free Trade Agreement.

Even before the current economic meltdown, the expendability of the most vulnerable is easily documented on the domestic scene as well: thousands of children in the United States without health care or coverage; 28 million Americans receiving food stamps; increasing numbers of seniors having to choose each month between groceries, rent payments, or health care; more and more citizens, including the working poor and now middle-class Americans, flocking to food banks. The outsourcing of American jobs to more profitable locations abroad inevitably sacrifices the well-being of a growing number of Americans. Tax breaks for the wealthy and greater disparity between rich and poor are signs of empire's preferential option for the powerful and the privileged. Human sacrifice is about both physical death and quality of life. Hopefully some of these trends may be in a process of reversal or amelioration under the present U.S. administration. Time will tell. Be that as it may, how can the church address these conditions?

U.S. Culture and Church Culture

In his book, *The Limits of Power,* Andrew J. Bacevich reflects on what he calls the crisis of profligacy. In defining what it means to be an American in the twenty-first century, he writes, "If one were to choose a single word to characterize that identity, it would have to be *more.* For the majority of contemporary Americans, the essence of life, liberty, and the pursuit of happiness centers on a relentless personal quest to acquire, to consume, and to shed whatever restraints might interfere with those endeavors."[1]

In light of the present economic debacle, Bacevich's analysis rings true. Our whole system of consumerism and almost unlimited credit and resulting debt describes our present cultural condition with pinpoint accuracy. He goes on to say, "It would be misleading to suggest that every American has surrendered to this ethic of self-gratification. Resistance to its demands persists and takes many forms. Yet dissenters, intent on curbing the American penchant for consumption and self-indulgence, are fighting a rear guard action, valiant perhaps but unlikely to reverse the tide. The ethic of self-gratification has firmly entrenched itself as the defining feature of the American way of life."[2]

What are we as the Church to say and do about this? I expect many of us would instantly claim that there are plenty of our church members whose faith and action arise above the seemingly secular terrain described by Bacevich. True enough.

Yet is it not the case that strong religious and cultural factors militate against "standing apart from the crowd" and thus against the prophetic ministry required to pursue justice? The widespread belief of a religious savior as the guarantor or at least the avenue of personal salvation above all else does not lend itself to improving the present world in ways that require self-denial on behalf of others. The cultural reality of "more" as described by Bacevich is tied to an alliance with capitalism in which success means either growth or bigger is better. The support of the

Iraq War by most of our churches, or at least the lack of strong church dissent, reveals a nationalism of greater weight than allegiance to the Prince of Peace. How, then, can the church become free enough to move towards the vocation of justice in spite of its cultural context?

In Chapter 3, I will suggest a number of strengths or means of grace for moving beyond cultural captivity. My intent therein is to reframe some of God's basic gifts in a manner that empowers the vocation of justice. Chapters 4 and 5 offer concrete examples of taking on justice issues in various settings in ways defying or at least challenging popular church culture.

Another approach in grappling with societal and church culture comes from the work of the late Edwin H. Friedman, rabbi and therapist. His earlier works, *Generation to Generation* and *Friedman's Fables*, are now further articulated in *A Failure of Nerve: Leadership in the Age of the Quick Fix*. He sets forth a clear conviction that significant change in any organization or community is best accomplished by what he calls a well-differentiated leader: "Differentiation is charting one's own way by means of one's own internal guidance system, rather than perpetually eyeing the 'scope' to see where others are at."[3]

Other nuances of the well-defined leader are described thusly: "Someone who can be separate while still remaining connected, and therefore can maintain a modifying, non-anxious and sometimes challenging presence ... Someone who can manage his or her own reactivity to the automatic reactivity of others, and therefore be able to take stands at the risk of displeasing."[4]

If these all too brief descriptions introduce you to Friedman and spark your imagination and curiosity, I encourage you to read *A Failure of Nerve*. Or if you are familiar with Friedman's work, you may wish to return to it for a fresh reading. If nothing else, his approach invites people in places of responsibility to exert more energy in changing oneself than in fixing others. Friedman's experience and observations as a therapist and counselor have led him to believe in leaders whose main job is self-understanding rather than in understanding data and improving technique.

Friedman encourages leaders to "develop a support system outside of the work system; stay focused on long-term goals; practice deep breathing, prayer, or meditation; listen to your body; and keep the system loose through humor."[5]

We turn now to biblical signs of justice.

Biblical Signs of Prophetic Spirit

The Hebrew bible contains a vast array of stories and historical contexts over several centuries in which the prophetic spirit of justice is narrated. In this chapter I have chosen to reflect on just three examples of justice. One is from the Torah as an early sign, and the other two are from Amos and Third Isaiah.

When I ask church groups if they know the biblical story of Shiphrah and Puah, I usually get blank stares. Their extended story is about five women of courage and ingenuity. Not only that, it's a tale of prophetic spirit and cooperation transcending the enmity of their ethnically diverse Hebrew and Egyptian backgrounds.

Let's begin with Exodus 1:15. The King of Egypt (Pharaoh), fearing the Israelites' growing strength in spite of severe oppression laid upon them, instructs two Hebrew midwives, Shiphrah and Puah, to kill the male infants born to Hebrew women. The scene is reminiscent of Herod in Matthew 2. The birth stool is to serve as a killing field for Hebrew sons, but the daughters are to be allowed to live (one place in Scripture where females get a break!). But, we are told, the midwives feared God, disobeyed the King, and let the male infants live. When questioned by the irate King, the midwives claim the Hebrew women, unlike the Egyptian women, are vigorous and give birth before the midwives can arrive on the scene. God blesses the midwives and the Israelites multiply in strength. Since the birth stool strategy fails, Pharaoh unleashes a second commandment in the national interest. Newborn Hebrew male infants are to be cast into the Nile and presumably not heard from again. In our time it's been called extraordinary rendition.

The midwives' decision to thumb their noses at the King is a triumph of faith. "But the midwives feared God." Perhaps it's an accident of translation but "But" indicates a shift in consciousness, an awareness of an alternative choice. The prophetic instinct, inspiration, and implementation begin with a "But,' that is, a sense of discrepancy between what is and what could and should be. For Shiphrah and Puah, God was the "But" giver. "But" is the forerunner of truth telling, resistance, and subversion in God's name. We encounter God's "But" again in Acts 5. The apostles are sternly warned not to teach in Jesus' name. "But," Peter and the apostles answered, "we must obey God rather than men" (5:29). We also see resistance from Shadrach, Meshach, and Abednego to King Nebuchadnezzar. The three troublemakers say that their God may deliver them from the fiery furnace, "But if not, be it known to you, O King, that we will not serve your gods, and we will not worship the golden statue that you have set up" (Daniel 3:17-18). Shiphrah and Puah are not named among the Hebrew prophets, but I think of them as among the earliest biblical progenitors and predecessors of prophetic spirit by which justice is served.

Biblical scholar Walter Brueggemann offers this cogent insight regarding the narrative: "In this dangerous mix of power and powerlessness, the narrative places Shiphrah and Puah. Amazing. They are nowhere else named or known, and certainly not celebrated. Yet we remember them by name. We remember these two discreet, defiant, cunning, mothering agents. At great risk they counter genocide; in so doing, they bear witness to the mothering power of God, whose will for life overrides the killing, and whose power for life is undeterred by the death dispensed by the powerful."[6]

In Exodus 2:1-10 three more women enter the narrative. The text tells us a Hebrew man from the house of Levi marries a Levite woman. She conceives and gives birth to a son. For three months the mother hides her son as protection against Pharaoh's murderous edict. When she can no longer hide her son, she prepares a basket, puts the infant in it, and places it among the reeds on the bank of the river Nile. Standing in the distance the child's sister quietly observes the placement.

Soon thereafter Pharaoh's daughter, intending to bathe in the river, discovers the child. In a mood of compassion she surmises that the infant must be one of the Hebrew children. Once again the boy's sister is on hand, this time offering to secure a nurse from among the Hebrew women to nurse the child. We might conclude that the infant's sister was adept at practicing a ministry of humane opportunity, being at the right place at the right time, not once but twice.

At this point in the narrative the two women, one the Egyptian daughter of Pharaoh, and the other the child's Hebrew sister, enter into a boundary-breaking covenant. Instead of following the wish of her father Pharaoh to destroy the child, she agrees to let the child be nurtured and raised by a Hebrew woman chosen, as it turns out and unbeknown to Pharaoh's daughter, by the child's sister. Although Pharaoh's daughter could have imposed harsh conditions, she even agrees to pay wages for the nurturing of the child to assure the child's future. And wouldn't we know by now, the Hebrew woman chosen as nurse by the wise and crafty sister turns out to be the child's mother and, of cours her own mother.

Years pass until the child grows up. The bargain between Pharaoh's daughter and the child's sister is completed when the mother returns her son to Pharaoh's daughter. She takes him as her own son and names him Moses. Four women from a people in slavery and one privileged woman within empire consorted and cooperated to preserve life against more improbabilities than we can imagine. Not the least of several ironies is that the Nile River, sought by Pharaoh as an instrument of death for male Hebrew babies, turns out to be the life-saving location for the one who was to become known as the liberator of the Hebrew people from slavery in Egypt. Without the willingness to take risks and to break through the usual restraints of cultural and family expectations by five courageous and politically astute women, there would have been no liberator named Moses. They provide early biblical signs of a prophetic spirit necessary to subvert empire and to rescue and restore life.

Notice that God is not mentioned as an agent in the unfolding plot of Exodus 2:1-10. According to Brueggemann, "The narrator has wrought a powerful interface between the hiddenness of God and the daring visibility of the women. One might conclude that the women act out of the hidden providence of God."[7]

Every contemporary effort on behalf of justice begins with a God-given "But" based on a sense of discrepancy, and for Christians, allegiance to the God of Shiphrah and Puah.

Connecting 8th to 6th Century B.C.E. Justice to Today

For Christians today the signs of justice in a generic sense lift up better quality of life and opportunity for all; more equitable sharing of the world's resources; freedom of speech, freedom from exploitation and abuse; and equal treatment under the law. The term social justice points to securing the well being and dignity of every member of the community with concern for the common good and for creation itself. Social justice is about equal access to all rights and privileges afforded by a society and, finally, about responsibilities as well. Even these rather general descriptions have profound implications for racial, gender, and class equality.

These are highly complex issues calling for analysis of how systems work, how they became the way they are, and how a greater measure of justice can become a reality. What is clear is the prophetic concern of justice, to use a biblical term, for sojourners, widows, and orphans. In contemporary terms, this translates into justice for the powerless, the marginalized, and the oppressed.

We preachers often tend to use the term justice or social justice as a catch-all term, almost like a magical mantra with little specificity or nuance. We shouldn't expect the laity to comprehend our meaning when we as preachers are not too clear in our own understanding. There are a number of interrelated justice issues such as commutative justice, environmental or ecological justice, and international justice, the latter two in particular having become more significant in our day. It's worth noting that different writers and social analysts vary in nomenclature and classification when weighing in on justice issues. The following paragraphs will consider two forms of justice basic to the prophets' message and to contemporary society.

When we scan the terrain of the 8th to 6th century B.C.E. Hebrew prophets, we become aware of a bewildering variety of contexts in which "the word of the Lord" is perceived and proclaimed. Two very specific forms of justice and righteousness often come to the surface, namely, procedural and distributive justice. I find these helpful in assisting some Christian laity to gain a firmer grasp of justice in the biblical sense. Sometimes these are referred to as legal and economic justice.

In his book *The Scandal of Evangelical Politics*, Ronald J. Sider provides a clear and concise description for us to consider: "Procedural justice defines the procedure that must be fair if justice is to prevail. Procedural justice requires such things as a transparent legal framework; unbiased courts; the rule of law; freedom of speech, assembly, and the vote; and honest elections … Distributive justice refers to how the numerous goods of society are divided. What is a just division of money, health care, educational opportunities – in short, all the goods and services in society." [8]

I have chosen passages from two Hebrew prophets as expressions of their concern for both procedural and distributive justice. Amos, prophet to the Northern Kingdom of Israel in the middle of the 8th century B.C.E., addresses God's judgment on greed and corruption involving both procedure and distribution. Israel has betrayed God's covenant and will face the consequences of communal disintegration or exile: "Woe to you who turn judgment into bitterness and do no justice in the land. You hate him who reproves in court; you despise him who speaks the truth. Because you have trampled on the poor man and extorted levies on his grain, though you have built mansions of hewn stones you will not dwell in them; though you have planted choice grapevines, you shall not drink of their wine. For I know the number of your crimes and how grievous are your sins; persecuting the just, taking bribes, turning away the needy at the gates." (Amos 5:7-12, from *The Christian Community Bible*)

The concerns of fair courts and reliable judicial officials are also expressed in the Torah (see Ex. 18:13-23, 23:6-8; Deut. 1:16-17, 16:18-20).

The 58th chapter of Isaiah redefines Israel's worship in terms of both procedural and distributive justice. As in many passages in prophetic literature, both judgment and hope are proclaimed as God's word. God's intent is what we can call restorative justice, that is, to restore the Hebrew people to covenant faithfulness. Thus, God's justice is more than economic equity or a transparent legal system. At the heart of God's justice is God's loving kindness (*hesed*) in the Hebrew bible intended to restore community for the common good. In the New Testament God's love through Jesus Christ calls forth restoration and reconciliation basic to true community. Simply put, God's call to justice is the sign and seal of God's love. This Isaiah text is true to this purpose.

In this passage Israel has returned from exile with no clear vision for the future. Gloom settles over the community. Somewhat in desperation the people, seeking to gain God's attention and favor, enter into a fast, humbling themselves with sackcloth and ashes: "Why do we fast, but you do not see? Why humble ourselves, but you do not notice?"

God's response seeks to return Israel to its true vocation of being a just and righteous people: "Look, you serve your own interest on your fast day, and oppress all your workers ... such fasting as you do today will not make your voice heard on high ... will you call this a fast acceptable to the Lord?"

"Is this not the fast that I choose: to loose the bonds of injustice, to undo the thongs of the yoke, to let the oppressed go free, and to break every yoke? Is it not to share your bread with the hungry and bring the homeless poor into your house; when you see the naked, to cover them, and not to hide yourself from your own kin?"

"Then your light shall break forth like the dawn, and your healing shall spring up quickly ... then you shall call, and the Lord will answer; you shall cry for help and he will say, Here I am ... the Lord will guide you continually, and satisfy your needs in parched places, and make your bones strong; and you shall be like a watered garden, like a spring of water, whose waters never fail."

"Your ancient ruins shall be rebuilt; you shall raise up the foundations of many generations; you shall be called the repairer of the breach, the restorer of streets to live in." (excerpts from verses 3-12)

There is a major shift of Israel's worship as practiced in this text from strictly a cultic act to a compassionate one, from self-absorption in sackcloth and ashes to an ethical vocation. More specifically, what strikes me in the text is the remarkable range of concern for both procedural and distributive justice. It connects with our society in multiple ways:

Workers' rights, and by implication, fair wages and safe working conditions.

Justice for the poor, that is, the hungry, the homeless and those without adequate clothing.

Indirectly, concern for adequate health care, inevitably connected with working conditions, hunger, and homelessness.

Implications for a peaceful society, or *shalom,* based on just structures.

What is especially clear is that God expects not just charity but that justice be built in to Israel's common life. The text speaks clearly of undoing and breaking of every yoke and letting the oppressed go free. Theologian Joerg Rieger reminds us that "divine judgment is the last remaining hope of those who are wronged, who are trampled under foot."[9] I think of this Isaiah text as something of a companion narrative with Matthew 25:31-46, often referred to as the Parable of the Last Judgment (the NRSV subheading is The Judgment of the Nations). Both speak to systems as well as to individuals and both have consequences to consider.

Several issues arising from these texts and from Christian experience deserve our attention. I call it idealism and realism informing each other:

1. God takes sides as clearly shown in biblical texts. Christian justice vocation starts with God's "side-taking" and attempts to honor it in public and personal life.

2. Justice vocation, whether addressing procedural or distributive realities, is usually messy, complex, and not given to perfection. Contingent, proximate, and ambiguous results are often more likely.

3. Matters of procedural and distributive justice are innately political in nature because they are all about power arrangements and the consequences of these arrangements.

4. Procedural and distributive justice inevitably demand racial justice, gender justice, and sexual identity justice.

5. Human rights are indispensable to justice but are at their best in honoring the common good lest they become too narrowly focused. It's all about all of us.

Faith and Politics

Many of us have grown up with the admonition "religion and politics don't mix." The assumption seems to be that religion is a separate sphere of its own not related to the great issues of the world. Or that politics is so degrading or "secular" that we do well to leave it alone. Or that taking on religion and politics in certain family conversations results in more cussing than discussing and is best avoided.

If you were to write an outline of your beliefs about faith and politics, what would it look like? What follows are some questions and thoughts which have been useful for me in providing a sense of direction and guidance connecting my faith and politics. Each invites further insight and discussion:

1. I do my best to connect political activity and decisions with my understanding of the mind and heart of Jesus. What were and are his priorities? Where was his preferential option of special concern? Where do I connect with the tradition from which Jesus emerged, namely, the prophets of social justice?

2. Political engagement is a key way I seek to love my neighbor in a collective sense. Personal contacts, as important as they are, are limited to a relatively few persons. I can reach out to thousands, most of whom I may never see or meet, by working for a Civil Rights Act or a law providing equal rights to gays and lesbians on a state or national level.

3. Reflection on political decision-making is not about political correctness or incorrectness but about theological faithfulness. What decisions and priorities honor or best represent Jesus' life and ministry?

4. Public policy decisions impact our lives in so many important ways from health care to educational priorities, human rights, religious freedom, taking care of the infrastructure of highways and bridges. How, then, can we as Christians not be involved in the political arena?

5. Conscientious Christians cannot turn over politics to just anyone who comes along. This is admittedly an extreme example, but I've never forgotten the story of Hitler's directive to the German church. He told the church leaders to take care of spiritual needs and he would take care of the political order.

6. Politics is about how power is organized, controlled, and utilized. The vocation of justice is inevitably connected with political values as they impinge on legal, economic, and environmental matters.

7. I have long believed "if you want peace, work for justice." I like to add, "and if you want justice, work for humane political decisions serving the common good." For Christians our public policy priority should be the well being of the most vulnerable among us.

8. Christian clergy have a responsibility to assist church members to think biblically and theologically about political action, and at the same time to learn from politically knowledgeable laity.

9. Political decision-making has to do with how a community organizes itself, how it makes decisions, who is at the table, who decides, who benefits, and what are the consequences.

10. Faith and politics combine to define the common good and to evaluate the competing claims for recognition and realization..

Chapter 3 provides a supportive bridge from understanding the source and signs of justice to the active seeking and doing justice in Chapters 4 and 5.

Notes

[1] Andrew J. Bacevich, *The Limits of Power*, Holt and Company, 2008, p. 16.
[2] Ibid.
[3] Edwin H. Friedman, *A Failure of Nerve*, Seabury Press, an imprint of Church Publishing, Inc., 1991 and 2007, p. 183.
[4] Friedman, p. 14.
[5] Friedman, p. 245.
[6] Brueggemann, *The New Interpreter's Bible*, Vol. 1, Abingdon Press, 1994, p. 697.
[7] Brueggemann, p. 701.
[8] Ronald J. Sider, *The Scandal of Evangelical Politics*, Baker Books, 2008, p. 103.
[9] Joerg Rieger, *The Progressive Christian*, Vol. 182, 2008.

Questions for Reflection and Discussion

1. What makes working for justice worthwhile?

2. What procedural and/or distributive justice issues need attention in your town or city? Nationally?

3. Why should Christians be informed on political issues? What do these issues have to do with Christian faith?

4. How are political issues connected with Jesus' life and ministry?

5. What do you see as the difference between social justice and social services?

CHAPTER 3

STRENGTH FOR JUSTICE

The Church is not ours to save or lose. It is God's gift to us.
Bishop Eugene Robinson

Draw near to God and God will draw near to you.
James 4:8

In the ninth chapter of Matthew's Gospel (9:18-33), the narrative presents Jesus the healer as the personification of the in-breaking Reign of God. Jesus restores life to a young girl. In other words Jesus comes calling forth life amid the conditions of death. A woman with a twelve-year hemorrhage is then made well. Jesus comes calling forth wholeness amid the conditions of sickness, community in the midst of isolation. Now come two blind men whose eyes were opened by Jesus. He calls forth sight amid the conditions of blindness. I don't rule out possible physical implications in the restoration of sight, but that's not the way we sing *Amazing Grace*; "I once was blind, but now I see" bears witness to life changing transformation.

By this time in the text you might imagine Jesus would be ready to call it a day. He's already had a busy day at the office which for him meant ministry in homes and on the street. But he's not through yet. There is a man who has no voice, or as the NRSV puts it, a demoniac who was mute. The demon of being without voice is cast out by Jesus. The text's description of the outcome is sublime in its simplicity: the man spoke. So it was, and so it is, Jesus comes calling forth voice amid the conditions of silence. The people's response? An amazed crowd exclaimed, "Never was anything like this seen in Israel." (vs. 33)

Our willingness and our capacity to embrace the vocation of justice depend on our receiving voice lessons from the God of the prophets and Jesus. Our demons of being voiceless, of being paralyzed by silence when truth needs to be spoken and acknowledged in action can be healed by God's voice finding expression in our voice. Isaiah in the temple (Is. 6) heard the voice of the Lord saying, "Whom shall I send, and who will go for us?" Then I said, "Here am I, send me!" Likewise, Jesus' baptism was immediately followed by a heavenly voice confirming his identity and mission.

The text is about more than God's voice lessons for those who seek to follow Jesus. God seeks to give universal voice lessons and especially to those who have had no voice, those who are disregarded by the Church and by the dominant culture. Vincent Harding, who teaches at Iliff School of Theology, said that the Church needs to practice listening to those who aren't supposed to have anything to say worth hearing. Sometimes the Church speaks best by listening and learning.

God's voice is wiser, more just, more dependable, more loving than all of our voices put together. God's voice may be heard in the wind and earthquake or through the still, small voice. Most important, God's voice abides for all time. The late Archbishop Oscar Romero of El Salvador reminds all of us who preach, "The Word remains. This is the great comfort of one who preaches. My voice will disappear, but my word, which is Christ, will remain."[1] And from Isaiah 40:8, "The grass withers, the flower fades, but the Word of our God will stand forever."

Here a major caveat is in order. No matter how diligent and discerning we hope to be, we can always misinterpret God's voice or bend it to suit our own preferences. Whether such misapplication be semi-conscious or hidden from ourselves, we need the insight and often the correction of others in the community of faith and sometimes beyond the pale of the faith. Even these are no guarantee that we interpret God's voice in a way conducive to God's intent and purpose. If we have learned anything from church history, we surely recognize the dangers of misusing what we claim to be God's voice and thus our need to proceed with humility and awe. If our interpretation of God's voice does not point to a God of love and justice, a God of truth and peace, and to our being called to respond accordingly, we'd best keep quiet and keep listening.

We are usually best empowered to receive God's voice lessons and to hear God's voice in others by staying close to the means of grace as variously defined, and by cultivating mentors whose lives, and sometimes martyrdom, have been especially devoted and faithful to the vocation of peace and justice. Means of grace bring to mind Word, water, wheat, wine, and other gifts of God now to be explored. What follows are some sources of strength which have sustained justice seeking and doing for generations of Christians, brought together through my own interpretation and experience.

The Written Word

Strength for justice often comes to us in the form of biblical texts. What better way for God's voice lessons to be heard than in the written Word in spite of the perils involved. To be sure, it's absolutely necessary to distinguish the poisonous passages that are harmful to human well being from the passages that promote God's life giving love. When I think about what factors have shaped my own justice learning and doing, I always come back to the many biblical texts that express justice as close to the heart of God. When biblical texts, carefully and wisely interpreted, become the cradle of our imagination, the context of our illumination, and the content of our implementation, there's no telling what God can bring about in terms of faithful advocacy for peace and justice.

There's a huge difference between taking on justice issues on one's own strength and embracing justice vocation with God's wind at our back. A biblically based justice orientation provides staying power and a sense of being a participant in God's purpose for creation. We're not best about justice through our own initiative or simply our own desire to make things right. Strength for justice in biblical texts comes as gift, blessing, challenge, and sometimes as ambiguity calling for meditation. Here are a few examples:

"He executes justice for the fatherless and the widow, and loves the sojourner, giving him food and clothing. Love the sojourner therefore; for you were sojourners in the land of Egypt." (Deut. 10:18)

27

"Righteousness and justice are the foundations of your throne; steadfast love and faithfulness go before you." (Ps. 89:14)

"Happy are those whose help is the God of Jacob, whose hope is in the Lord their God ... who executes justice for the oppressed, who gives food to the hungry." (Ps. 146:5-7)

"The Lord waits to be gracious to you; therefore he will rise up to show mercy to you. For the Lord is a God of justice; blessed are those who wait for him." (Is. 30:18)

"Seek God and not evil, that you may live; and so the Lord, the God of Hosts, will be with you ... hate evil and love good, and establish justice in the gate; it may be that the Lord, the God of hosts will be gracious to the remnant of Joseph." (Amos 5:14-15)

"Blessed are those who hunger and thirst for righteousness, for they will be filled." (Matt. 5:6)

"Blessed are the peacemakers, for they will be called the children of God." (Matt. 5:9)

In Isaiah 42, a vision of God's chosen servant is centered in a mission of bringing forth justice: "I have put my spirit upon him, he will bring forth justice to the nations ... he will not fail or be discouraged till he has established justice in the earth." (Is. 42:1-4, RSV) Matthew's gospel interprets this passage as a description of Jesus' ministry: "Here is my servant whom I have chosen ... I will put my Spirit upon him and he will proclaim justice to the Gentiles ... he will not break a bruised reed or quench a smoldering wick until he brings justice to victory. And in his name the Gentiles will hope ..." (Matt. 12:18-21)

Allow these texts and others like them to nourish and embolden our justice vocation as Christians.

The Proclaimed Word

I have long believed that preaching sets the tone for congregational life and mission. If we think of the church as being inherently prophetic rather than simply having a prophetic task, our sermons will provide strength for justice consistent with the God of peace and justice in whose name we preach. In a previous book, I wrote: "Peace with justice is not meant to be a sudden, jarring slogan from the pulpit; it should characterize our whole ministry. What should seem odd to parishioners is our silence from the pulpit on major questions of the day."[2]

From 1985 to 1993 I taught at Perkins School of Theology, SMU, through the LeVan Chair of Preaching and Worship. I encouraged students to preach at least one sermon on a contemporary social issue. Class discussion addressed questions like these: What does the Good News save people for? How can sermons reflect the social conscience of the Bible in today's congregational life? What is our basic paradigm of preaching from where people are to where the Gospel would lead us? What determines whether the preacher interprets the biblical text only for the perceived individual needs of church members or for larger and global issues as well? How can the pulpit strengthen the church's commitment to justice vocation?

Here are three homiletical guidelines I have found useful for myself and for students:

1. Pastoral ministry and prophetic sermons can reinforce each other and strengthen the total ministry of the congregation. Lay people inevitably respond to challenging sermons based on their experience of the preacher as a caring pastor and as an administrator who works respectfully with people, not around or above people. The persona of the pastor as one remembered at the hospital bedside and as a trusted confidant goes a long way in gaining an ear to the pulpit. I have hardly ever known an exception to this connection. The first lesson of prophetic preaching is not necessarily the content of the sermon but the relationship of the preacher/pastor to the congregation. When the ordained minister treats the pastoral and the prophetic as a seamless garment, laity will be encouraged to do the same. (See Appendix B for related treatment)

2. One of my patron saints will always be a ninety-year old woman who lived across the street from the parsonage in my first pastorate. Her name was Austa Wyrick. After one of my first sermons she said to me, "Young man, I have something to say to you." Naturally I thought, "Oh boy, I'm in for it now; gird your loins." She actually had a question and it was this: "In all my years as a church member, why have I not heard an enlightened biblical interpretation which I heard today? Why have those of us in the pew been so protected instead of challenged?" Many of my sermons have not elicited such favor. Somehow this one struck home in a positive way.

A pulpit consistently grounded in biblical passages can weave a fabric of theological discernment and discovery through which the congregation can grow towards new approaches and new questions. In our fearfulness we clergy too easily overlook the reality of hunger for deeper biblical knowledge and theological insight among the laity. Depriving the hope and hunger of the Austa Wyricks in our congregation is not a valid gospel option.

3. Humility combined with homiletical homework goes a long way in inviting our listeners into the sermon, even sermons addressing controversial matters. A confessional style communicates to the listener that the Gospel speaks to the preacher as well as the congregation. Long ago I became convinced of the wisdom and efficacy of an inquiring mode of prophetic preaching. Preacher and people are brought together as co-searchers for truth and insight.

Humility calls us as preachers to ask, "Why do some think the way they do, say, on immigration, military might, or race relations?" We thereby "exegete" our listeners' history and background, our own journey that has led us to believe as we do, and the values of the culture. People who are heard and hopefully understood are more likely to gravitate towards preaching that strengthens the church's justice ministry.

I'm not suggesting comfort-seeking compromise. I am suggesting a view of preaching beyond dogmatism, yet also beyond majority vote. Insofar as possible, I want to preach biblically and theologically so that I lead those who take offense into a deeper dialogue with scripture instead of having barbecued preacher for lunch!

Not along ago I was asked to be the preacher for a struggling congregation's annual service of renewal. After accepting the invitation, I was able to spend time in advance with the pastor and lay leaders listening and learning of the congregation's history and present situation. The congregation was experiencing declining membership and morale. Speaking as best I could into their context, my sermons tackled themes of centering in God's Word and cultivating the Word in response to God's initiating grace.

Proceeding from gift to challenge, from promise to claim, I suggested that the congregation was not too old, financially strapped, stuck in the past, fouled up by the previous pastor (as claimed by some), or too anything else to be unable to follow Jesus' example of love for each other and for others beyond the congregation.

None of these limits automatically prevents a congregation from loving God and neighbor or from seeking justice. Yes, it would be nice if we had more members, nice if we had more money, nice if we had a stable neighborhood, nice if we had more children and youth. Yes, it would be nice if ---------------. When the Word becomes front and center, congregational life has been known to break new ground, rediscover immense gratitude for God's "no-matter-what love" and become a place and a people generous in spirit and soul. That's why every congregation has the God-given potential for becoming a loving, justice seeking community.

The Watered Word

Images of baptism in the synoptic gospels and in Romans are on the wild side. Early on in Mark's gospel (1:4), there appears from nowhere in the Judean wilderness a locust and wild honey eating character wearing a leather belt and clothed in camel's hair. This one called John baptized the multitudes in the River Jordan, calling for repentance.

He also baptized Jesus. Not vice versa. Whatever we make of this, it's worth noting that Jesus was not baptized by a credentialed priest from the temple or for that matter by a representative of any religiously recognized establishment. Like so much of Jesus' ministry his baptism seems to suggest a reversal of commonly accepted wisdom and procedure. Instead we are given an alternative to ponder and question. The occasion takes on a cosmic aura as the heavens are torn asunder, the Spirit descends on Jesus like a dove as he emerges from the water, and a voice from heaven is said to affirm Jesus as son of the Divine.

Matthew and Luke offer similar accounts with some variations. In these narratives Jesus baptizes with both the Holy Spirit and fire and will come with winnowing fork as though to fulfill Simeon's claim that "this child is set for the fall and rising of many in Israel" (Luke 2:34).

Paul's version of baptism in Romans 6 is likewise disturbing to conventional wisdom and the practice of comfortable baptismal liturgy today. What could be more radical than baptism in Christ Jesus, which amounts to being baptized into his death (vs. 3). Paul speaks of being buried with Christ and being united with him in a resurrection like his.

If we take this imagery to heart, it has to be both scary and awesome in its promise and demand.

Throughout the Book of Acts baptism is experienced by an amazing diversity of people. They include large groups, men and women, an Ethiopian eunuch, Cornelius the centurion and other Gentiles, Lydia and her household, and a jailer and all his family. These scenes tell us that baptism is inclusive and is the common origin of Christians in scripture and historically in spite of differences in theology and practice.

Discernment for Today

The watered word proclaims God's already existing unconditional love. Contrary to cultural norms and expectations, God's love is not conditional on our worthiness, our understanding of Divine Grace, or anything in the future that we do or do not do. Baptism marks us for life as belonging to God. It is our identification card, a radical statement of identity. It's our spiritual, theological Master Card. We do well not to leave home without it.

Have you ever wondered why most languages capitalize I in a sentence while we is in lower case? The watered word reflects God's desire that we find our true selves in community yet retain our individuality. Some of us are fortunate enough to have found our I-We in Christian community although this is far from true for all too many persons who have longed for a safe, yet stretching community in the name of Jesus Christ.

When I turned 80 in June, 2008, I attempted to describe in the Northaven United Methodist Church Newsletter the I-We for which I have been most grateful: "Driving on Preston Road recently I saw a sign 'assisted living,' followed by a place name and phone number. The term assisted living conjures up images of decline, frailty, and dependency. In reality we have been indebted to assisted living since birth and even in our mother's womb. For many of us, our days have been characterized by the assistance, one way or another, from parents, family, friends, mentors, and a host of others. It happens in both individualized relationships and in more communal settings. I call this pervasive grace. This being said, I fully realize there are readers who have not experienced assisted living as positive as suggested above."

Continuing the message to Northaven UMC where I served as pastor from 1967-73, and where Fran and I have worshipped since 1985, I filled in some thoughts about assisted living in these words: "I can only give thanks to the Northaven community, as well as to others, for being a means of grace through countless acts of assisted living ... welcoming back a former pastor, providing opportunities for pastoral and prophetic ministry, putting up with my blind spots, offering a creative environment for growth, sharing each others hurts and hopes, and developing new friends.

"To share God's unconditional love together is an ultimate experience of assisted living. To be embraced by the Good News is to be touched by a mysterious Lover who brings all life into being; who affirms our worth in spite of our failures, offering new beginnings to all our endings; who undergirds the worst sinner with the offer of redeeming love and undermines the best hypocrite with judgment calling forth repentance; who beckons us to follow in the footsteps of the One sent to preach good news to the poor and recovering of sight to the blind, to bind up the brokenhearted, to set at liberty those who are oppressed; who invites us to be barrier breakers and community makers standing up for peace and justice; who gives no worldly guarantee of victory other than the victory of living for risk-filled truth itself. Assisted living indeed."

Baptism is God's way of calling forth the hope and actuality of the I-We in which our lives find their true identity in the community of faith, hope, and love. The watered word is not water or word of just any community or organization. Baptism proclaims God's calling the church to be shaped and formed by the mind and heart of Jesus. The watered word is God's radical invitation to be a participant in a stretching community of repentance and reconciliation, inquiry and illumination, love and liberation. These are roots in both John the Baptist and Jesus Christ. The watered word is God's earliest public call to a vocation of justice. The United Methodist baptismal liturgy names it this way in the section Renunciation of Sin and Profession of Faith: "Do you accept the freedom and power God gives you to resist evil, injustice, and oppression in whatever form they present themselves?" (The United Methodist Hymnal, p. 34) We are invited to remember this call by either faith memory in the case of infant baptism or by brain memory in the case of youth and adult baptism.

United Methodists usually sprinkle the watered word although we are allowed to pour or submerge. Having served a year as an interim minister in the Christian Church (Disciples of Christ), and having immersed several youths during an Easter baptism, I have to admit that you know for sure you have been baptized through the drama of "dying and rising with Christ." Seemingly primitive? Maybe so, maybe not. While the amount of water of course does not matter in one sense, immersion may be a more clear and dramatic sign of the radical intent of baptism in Christ. I must say that if we are going to baptize by sprinkling, let's have more prominent fonts than tiny bowls for which one has to look carefully to locate upon entering the sanctuary. Further, let's not fear to move beyond daintiness to messiness in the application of the watered word.

The watered word places a huge responsibility on pastors. Do we settle for a domesticated interpretation in preparing those to be baptized? Or do we make every effort to reveal this sacrament as a deep rite of passage recognizing both the promise and the claim of the Crucified and Risen Christ? The priesthood of all believers is rooted in baptism by which all Christians are called to be ministers of Jesus Christ.

Wheat and Wine

What's going on when Christians partake of the Eucharist, also known as the Lord's Supper or Holy Communion?

Sometimes we experience an overwhelming sense of gratitude and joyful thanksgiving in response to God's grace. Some worshippers describe a deepening personal relationship with Jesus Christ, a real or spiritual presence that gives strength in times of tribulation. Still others come to the sacrament with repentance and discover God's healing forgiveness, thus laying down a burden and receiving a fresh beginning. The deep sense of communal sharing of the bread and cup in a closely-knit congregation is frequently mentioned. All of these accounts have roots in biblical and historical precedents. And all are rooted in the conviction that the sacrament is deeply personal and pastoral. I have become fond of saying that if all else fails, receive the Eucharist of God's unconditional love.

In recent years I have become convinced that the Eucharist is not only a profound personal experience with God through Jesus Christ, but also a sacrament of profound public and prophetic implications. Indeed, I have come to believe the public and prophetic significance of the Eucharist may well be the best kept secret in the North American Church. Almost never do I hear U.S. Christians, regardless of which tradition or denomination, speak of Holy Communion as a sacrament of God's justice.

The Eucharist as Public and Prophetic

Eucharist a strength for the vocation of justice? Holy Communion connected with public policy? The Lord's Supper a call to prophetic action? By all means. But how so?[3] To affirm the prophetic and public dimensions of the Eucharist is in no way to deny the personal and pastoral features. Communion narratives in 1 Corinthians 10 and 11 and in the synoptic gospels (Matt. 26, Mark 14, and Luke 22 and 24) have been the source of Christian observance and celebration for centuries. Both pastoral and prophetic interpretations are embedded in these remembrances.

To unveil the connection between Eucharist and justice, that is, the public and prophetic, I will begin with contemporary narratives and then retrace a path to the biblical authority.

Contemporary Connections

Jim Wallis, known to many through his speaking, writing, and Sojourners Magazine, tells a story dramatically connecting the Eucharist with justice. He was visiting Holy Trinity Anglican Church in South London whereupon the rector pointed to an old, well-worn table in the sanctuary. When asked why it was so special, the rector indicated it was the table on which William Wilburforce wrote much of his anti-slavery legislation for the English parliament and the table used every Sunday by the congregation for communion.[4]

A twenty-year relationship between Northaven United Methodist Church in Dallas and Maria Madre de los Pobres in El Salvador has brought forth a strong awareness of justice and Eucharist. In worshipping with our friends in Maria Madre it became clear that the Eucharist breathed the hope for a better life of peace, justice, and truth. It was not by accident that Archbishop Romero was assassinated in worship while celebrating the Eucharist. The dominant powers in El Salvador were theologically bankrupt but not theologically naïve. They realized the Eucharist was a threat that provided hope to the people.

In 1988 I heard a sermon by Fr. Molina in a Franciscan church in Managua, Nicaragua. The text was Mark 1:40-42. Since the sermon there is always in the context of the Eucharist, we might say every sermon is a eucharistic sermon. In the text a leper approaches Jesus seeking to be healed. As with many of the New Testament healing stories, touch and spoken word are the healing agents used by Jesus. The leper was made clean. The healer who liberates the leper, Molina said, is forever marginalized by fearful powers and principalities.

I expect it's fair to say that perhaps the majority of preachers in North America would declare the Good News to be Jesus' care for individuals, especially those in dire need such as the leper. The Lord of life makes time for all persons, touching their lives where the hurt is greatest. This is true to the Gospel. For Fr. Molina the leper was the embodiment of more than one individual. The leper represented all the *campesinos* of Latin America, all those marginalized by political and military power. His sermon embraced the social reality of the people. When the people participate in the communion, there is solidarity of preached and enacted Word bringing the hope of justice to each and all.

Through the centuries Christians have spoken in various ways of the eucharistic bread as the body of Christ and the wine or chalice as the blood of Christ. In whatever way we theologize about Christ's presence in the eucharistic elements, literally or symbolically, the Eucharist holds before us the vocation of peace and justice embodied in the life, death, and resurrection of Jesus Christ. The Eucharist is inherently justice oriented.

In his book *Spirituality and Liberation*, Robert McAfee Brown reflects on how bread and wine come to be: " The bread and wine are available only because there has been planting, cultivating, harvesting, gathering, fermenting or baking, storing, transporting, distributing, buying, and selling--in short, all those things we identify with the life of economics and politics.[5]

When we consider the eucharistic elements as inseparable from Jesus, the bread and wine say to us: "We call you to covenant community. We represent the world of commerce and trade and labor practices as God wants them to be. We come from God; now offer us back to the God of justice."

My friend Ruben Habito has helped me to see the bread and chalice from an ecological standpoint in a similar way that Robert McAfee Brown has lifted up a political and economic understanding. Bread and wine can only come to fruition through soil, rain, sunshine, wind, and photosynthesis. Again, the bread and wine, in whatever form, say to us, "We represent the interaction of God's creation. Treasure this incomparable gift. Preserve it. Love it. Learn from it and live fruitfully. Fail to honor it and die fitfully." The Eucharist connects us with the earth and calls forth environmental justice and sustainability.

If we do not see God or Christ in human labor, in economics, in politics, in the created order represented by bread and wine, we have consigned God to our sanctuaries apart from daily life and struggle. Tissa Balasuriya, a Sri Lankan theologian, expressed a similar concern in saying, "The Eucharist has been domesticated within the dominant social establishment of the day. Its radical demands have been largely neutralized."[6]

Now we can begin to retrace the path of biblical authority giving credibility to contemporary experiences of Eucharist as public and prophetic.

The Emmaus Narrative

The Emmaus experience narrated in Luke 24:13-35 offers an implied connection with justice vocation. At Emmaus the Last Supper became the Everlasting Supper. As Martin Luther declared in *A Mighty Fortress is Our God,* "the body they may kill; God's truth abideth still." The Everlasting Supper is "a living enactment of the reign of God personified in Jesus. As such the Eucharist holds before us a vision of a world made whole and a people unified in peace, justice, and love. The Eucharist points to the renewal of the social order where there is enough to eat for everyone, where all stand or kneel on the equal ground of divine grace and thus the ground of worth and dignity."[7]

The Synoptic-Passover Narrative

The Emmaus story cannot be understood apart from its predecessor in the Upper Room told in Matthew 26, Mark 14, and Luke 22. The Upper Room meal narrated in these accounts is widely connected by scholars to the Jewish Passover meal. The latter event recalls the liberation of the Hebrews from slavery under Pharaoh. Likewise the Supper of the Lord is a meal of liberation. To partake of "the body and the blood" is to identify and grow in solidarity with the barrier breaker community maker, the champion of the poor, the Prince of Peace, the defender of justice. The Supper is thus meant to be an agent of formation in the mind and heart of Jesus.

The Eucharist is more than a call to justice but it cannot be less. We don't remember or partake of just anyone in the Lord's Supper. The action is tied to a specific life and person whom we call Lord. The late Frederick Herzog thought of the Eucharist in this way: "What we have in the Eucharist is a community gathering at God's behest to embody the character of God. In this community Messiah Jesus as the host personifies the mystery of God righting our human condition at its deepest level."[8]

The Earliest Narrative

From the synoptic narratives we link the eucharistic experience with Paul's account in I Corinthians 11, generally considered to be the earliest New Testament witness to the communal meal. All of the testimonies in the synoptic gospels and in 1 Corinthians utilize the fourfold action of taking bread, giving thanks, breaking it, and giving it to the disciples. The same formula holds for the feeding of the multitudes in Mark 6 and 8 and at Emmaus in Luke 24.

Paul insists that those who arrive ahead of others be respectful and wait for those who come later. The more affluent members were apparently able to come earlier than working class members. The lack of consideration for others did not do justice in Paul's mind to the intent of the Supper.

The theme of justice in the form of equality and inclusive procedure often appears in the New Testament without the term justice being used. Paul's admonition in 1 Corinthians is an example. In effect he is saying the Corinthians cannot rightly observe the meal of Jesus if some members are disregarded. Message and practice need to be a unity. As we all know, at least in our heads, a church that does not practice justice internally is a poor witness for justice externally.

Thoughts for Today

Living the Eucharist in today's world means that as eucharistic Christians we insist on the absolute inclusivity of the table sacrament for all who wish to be present in faith. Jesus is the host and has already set the rules for the table. Likewise we become advocates "in learning" with all those for whom God's justice is not a present reality.

For me to live the Eucharist means that, dependent on the grace, forgiveness, and power of God, I, a senior citizen white male, am called to be a faithful advocate in word and deed for the rights and well being of children, persons with disabilities, gays, lesbians, bisexuals, and transgender persons, people of color, women, refugees, and prisoners, among others. Living the Eucharist means that our liberation is bound up together, and that my attempts at justice advocacy depend not only on the grace of God but also on the wisdom and experience of those with whom I hope to be a friend and advocate.

I can count on the Eucharist, quite apart from the skill or lack thereof on the part of the preacher/liturgist to lift up Christ crucified and risen, to proclaim the gift and claim of God's justice to all who ingest the elements. The Eucharist will not provide easy answers to social justice issues, but it does hold up a vision of what might be and should be. Make no mistake, there are times when my faith is weak or lazy, so that I'm not sure I hear the justice orientation of the Eucharist as Good News. Isn't it just like God to wrestle us into places we'd just as soon not go? Perhaps that's precisely when the Eucharist becomes both deeply personal and deeply prophetic. Once again the Everlasting Supper embraces me with the meaning of my life ... to love mercy, to do justice, and to walk humbly with God. The wheat and wine of the Lord's Supper offers empowerment for a justice seeking people.

Corporate Worship

Liturgy, the way we worship God, sows seeds in the soil of the soul. Liturgy of silence, song, scripture, sermon, and sacrament, all undergirded by prayer and presence of the people, weaves a corporate autobiography defining the life of the congregation. At its best liturgy remembers and rehearses the church's sacred story.

During the Protestant Reformation liturgy became the work of the people. How different it must have been to worship in one's own language instead of Latin and to hear both scripture and sermon in native tongue. The people sang psalms and hymns and received both bread and cup in Holy Communion. In this sense, with some variations from place to place and reformer to reformer, the work of the people meant participation in worship.

However, liturgy as the work of the people means more than participation during the time of corporate worship. Liturgy is more than a printed order or resource to be used and discarded. In its most profound sense liturgy as the work of the people means the faithful presence of Christians in the world, practicing the liturgy of confession, celebration, and commitment as a way of life in the community, at work, at home, and yes, in the church. The liturgy provides a script for living the faith in the world, providing our marching orders so to speak.

When we connect liturgy with the way we are called to live in the world, the liturgical language, metaphors, and images in their various manifestations become highly significant. Are there prophetic images in word and artistic expression of a church called "to preach good news to the poor and to set at liberty those who are oppressed"? (from Luke 4, by way of Is. 61) Does worship enhance justice seeking? Does the liturgy, whether spoken, written, or sung stretch the congregation towards fresh visions of God's sometimes disturbing love?

The term "justice" of course has no magical effect in and of itself. Yet since words do shape reality and priorities for the church, the content of scripture passages, sermons, and hymns do give direction for the congregation's reason for being. Corporate worship can be a time and place where the seeds of justice are sown in the soil of the soul.

Here's a challenge for readers of any and all religious traditions. Examine your Orders of Service, your worship resources, looking for peace and justice oriented liturgy. What do you find? United Methodists, review the Basic Pattern of Worship and the Baptismal Covenant. How could the liturgy more faithfully reflect Jesus' ministry of justice?

During worship some congregations regularly hear a "mission minute" offered by one or more members of the congregation, thus informing the worshippers of the congregation's outreach in a particular instance. This practice alerts the congregation of "being for the world" and sometimes recruits other members for justice orientation and involvement.

For United Methodists the largest and clearest statements related to social justice are contained in our Social Principles rather than in our worship services. The Preface to the Social Principles reads: "The United Methodist Church has a long history of concern for social justice. Its members have often taken forthright positions on controversial issues involving Christian principles. Early Methodists expressed their opposition to the slave trade, to smuggling, and to the cruel treatment of prisoners." (Page 95, The Book of Discipline of The United Methodist Church, 2004)

To give non-Methodist readers a sense of the Social Principles, they speak to issues in sections titled The Natural World, The Nurturing Community, The Social Community, The Economic Community, The Political Community, The World Community. The Social Principles conclude with Our Social Creed (pp. 96 -125). The Principles are both gift and judgment for United Methodists. Given John Wesley's deep concern for the plight of the most vulnerable plus the content of our Social Principles, my United Methodist colleagues, both clergy and laity, and I have the least excuse of all Christian traditions to be negligent toward the vocation of justice.

If we think of the main weekly service of worship as the gathering of all the ministers of the church, at least those present on a given Sunday, we have a bold concept of ministerial potential that God can agitate, motivate, levitate, and celebrate for doing justice, loving mercy, and walking humbly with Divine Presence.

Spiritual Intentionality

Faithful commitment to spiritual disciplines or exercises often provides strength for justice ministry. The testimony of Christians through the centuries confirms the connection of justice efforts with the practice of discernment, meditation, prayer, scripture reading, fasting, and similar acts of renewal.

I have already stated that biblical texts are high in my experience of spiritual or faith formation. Silence is also a friend and is a frequent visitor in my life. I have practiced intentional seeking of mentors in various areas of life and ministry as a spiritual discipline. Here are a few notions of prayer that have nurtured me and strengthened my resolve for justice vocation:

1. Thy kingdom come, thy will be done on earth as it is in heaven (arguably the most radical of all Christian prayers).

2. Aligning myself and the community of faith with the presence and will of God. (learned from Dietrich Bonhoeffer)

3. Readiness and willingness to receive and appropriate the Word, and to accept it in one's personal situation, particular tasks, decisions, sins, and temptations. (also from Bonhoeffer)

4. Praying with your feet in vigils and peace rallies, as well as with our hearts and minds. (from Rabbi Abraham Heschel)

5. There is finally only one prayer and it has two words: Thank you. (from 13th century mystic Meister Eckhart)

Pablos for Peace and Justice

An artist with a conscience cannot separate himself from certain political issues. Chief among those issues are justice and freedom ...
I am a man first, an artist second ... my contribution to world peace (through music) may be small. But at least I will have given all I can to an ideal I hold sacred.
Pablo Casals[9]

In 1973 a military coup led by General Augusto Pinochet took control of Chile, overthrowing the constitutionally elected government of Salvador Allende with the support of the U.S. Central Intelligence

Agency. Referring to a search of his house and grounds at Isla Negra by the Chilean armed forces, Pablo Neruda remarked:

Look around – there's only one thing of danger for you here – poetry.
Pablo Neruda[10]

In the panel on which I am working, which I shall call Guernica, and in all my recent works of art, I clearly express my abhorrence of the military caste which has sunk Spain in an ocean of pain and death.
Pablo Picasso[11]

Guernica, a small village in the Basque area of Spain, was obliterated by German bombers in April, 1937 during the Spanish Civil War. It offered bombing practice for Hitler's air force in support of dictator Francisco Franco on the eve of World War II. The raid on Guernica was unparalleled in military history, killing hundreds of civilians whose village was not a military target. In just over three hours, the village and many of the people were destroyed by high explosives, incendiary bombs, and machine gun strafing in the nearby fields.

Pablo Picasso began painting his black and white mural in oil within fifteen days of the attack. In due time it became a prophetic vision of World War II, a protest of an unprecedented crime against humanity, and arguably modern art's most powerful anti-war statement. *Guernica* depicts human anguish with crying, screaming figures, including the mother with her dead child. The painting shows the destruction of humans, animals, and property. Theologian Paul Tillich stated that *Guernica* revealed the human situation without any cover, portraying a religious style or theme without religious content. The painting *Guernica* is now located in Madrid's Reina Sofia Museum.

These three Pablos, musician, poet, and painter/sculptor remind us that artists are often the most courageous and outspoken when tyranny overtakes a society. No wonder that the first citizens to be deposed by dictators are the poets, filmmakers, painters, sculptors, dancers, playwrights, and other artists who bring critical insight and judgment on the lies and pretensions of the enemies of freedom and justice. Even in death the truth tellers are a threat to tyranny. Pablo Neruda's funeral became the first public protest against the Chilean military dictatorship.

I have mentioned the three Pablos as a very small example of the countless artists, whether visual, literary, or performing, who have taken up the vocation of justice in dire circumstances. Those of us who are Christians owe a huge appreciation to many artists, some of whom are themselves Christians and to others who claim no active religious affiliation. Through the years I have found strength for justice through the courage of artists who often stand alone against oppression.

If you would like an educational and spiritual challenge, delve into recent histories of South Africa, El Salvador, Nicaragua, and other nations to discover the life and witness of artists who have followed the prophetic spirit, often with great sacrifice.

I don't want to leave the impression that artists are significant to us only because of speaking truth to power. In its various forms and expressions art can provide affirmation of life, deep insights into the human condition, grace in terms of beauty and blessing, a channel to the divine, as well as shedding light on church doctrine and history.

The church would be a very different community without the benefit of art. No architecture, no visual arts, no music, no dance or performing art. We do not usually think of scripture and sermon as art forms, yet these are efforts to communicate in written and spoken word, and for better or worse, are forms of artistic expression.

Give thanks for three Pablos, all of whom died in 1973, and for all whom they represent– past, present, and future.

Author's Note*:* In this chapter I have deliberately not mentioned small groups as basic to seeking justice. In Chapters 4 and 5, small groups will often be seen as the main agents in stories of justice sought and sometimes accomplished.

Notes

[1] James B. Brockman, *The Word Remains: A Life of Oscar Romero*, Orbis Books, 1982, cover.
[2] William K. McElvaney, *Preaching from Camelot to Covenant*, Abingdon Press, 1989, p, 58.

³A more thorough treatment of this claim is available *in Eating and Drinking at the Welcome Table*, William K. McElvaney, Chalice Press, 1998, pp. 51-70, and in "Embodying the Justice of God," *Zion's Herald*, (now *The Progressive Christian*), pp. 37-40, September/October, 2005.
⁴Paraphrased from Jim Wallis, *The Great Awakening*, Harper One, 2008,
p. 17.
⁵Robert McAfee Brown, *Spirituality and Liberation*, Westminster Press, 1988, p. 92.
⁶Tissa Balasuriya, *The Eucharist and Human Liberation*, Orbis Books, 1979, p. xi).
⁷William K. McElvaney, *Eating and Drinking at the Welcome Table*, Chalice Press, 1998, p. 64).
⁸Frederick Herzog, *God-Walk*, Orbis, 1988, p. 132).
⁹Albert Kahn, *Joys and Sorrows: Pablo Casals, His Own Story*, Simon and Schuster, 1970, pp. 208 and 286.
¹⁰*Pablo Neruda*, Wikipedia.
¹¹Colm Toibin, "The Art of War," *The Guardian*, April 29, 2006.

Questions for Reflection and Discussion

1. Which of these "strengths for justice" are most real to you and why?

2. How could the worship services of your congregation become more supportive of its justice vocation?

3. Is the notion of the Eucharist as a sacrament connected with social justice new to you? A group discussion on your memories and experiences of Holy Communion through the years can be lively and illuminating.

4. Here's a challenge: See if you can locate baptismal and eucharistic hymns that connect with the theme of justice or some dimension of social reform.

5. What "strengths for justice" have you experienced that are not included in Chapter 3?

SECTION II

DOING JUSTICE: ISSUES AND STRATEGIES

CHAPTER 4

PERSONAL DISCERNMENT AND DISCOVERY

If you are neutral in situations of injustice, you have chosen the side of the oppressor.

Archbishop Desmond Tutu

It isn't enough to love and pursue justice in God's name. We are also called to love and exercise mercy in God's name, even unto those whom we deem our enemies.

Cynthia Astle

A seminary student once described theological education as "having all your nerve endings exposed." So it is when injustice, and thus the need for justice, becomes clear. On the other hand, being grasped by God's call to justice as a vocation can be the discovery of a lifetime.

I can name three back and forth movements describing my Jacob-at-the-Jabbok wrestling match with God's call to justice. These are not like an automatic progression. No indeed, these movements wrestle with each other inside of me even today. I grew up in the church, but when I look back I have to name my initial dawning by the term "Duh." That's right, Duh. I'm using the term Duh in an opposite sense of the way it is often understood. Duh usually means "Everybody knows that." Here Duh means "I just don't get it." To this day there are faith issues that seem like Duh. Who among us escapes being theologically challenged, especially when the complexity of justice calls our name?

My justice path morphed from Duh to "Uh-Oh." I can pinpoint the time. For me it happened in seminary. Of course God's loose-in-the-world intervening grace can strike anyone anytime anywhere. The advent of a serious learning curve made itself known at the hands of some great teachers. My first real experience of critical theological reflection took hold. I began to ask, "Am I going in the direction I now believe God is calling me to go?" I discovered I'm more likely to leave Duh behind if and when I sense a discrepancy between where I am and where I need to go in the name of the Gospel. Uh-Oh is a combination of apprehension and anticipation. Does this touch your experience?

Out of Uh-Oh came "Aha." This began in seminary but took on greater clarity in pastoring my first two congregations in The United Methodist Church. It oozed from biblical texts from which I preached and became incarnate in the lives of people in the interchange of pastoral care. A Divine love that will not let us go. The most enduring values of life. Learning to love people I never dreamed of even caring about. Hoping to make life better for others. Understanding myself at a deeper level and embracing a confessional life as a spiritual practice. The Creator and Sustainer in the middle of it all. Not easy news. Not "here today gone tomorrow" news. Permanent Good News.

Almost imperceptibly Aha evolved into a more demanding faith realization. Over time I have called it by different names. For now it goes by the name of "Oh God." From Aha to Oh God. It's the stretch from charity to justice, from friendship to advocacy, from peacefulness to peacemaking. In my case great biblical texts and my growing awareness of people suffering from injustice merged to connect Aha with Oh God. I have told seminary students that it's something like a continental divide in ministry. Do you hear the ambivalence in Oh God? There's a measure of hesitancy and reticence. Am I up to this? Will God show the way? Doesn't justice often involve some measure of controversy and conflict? Yet in the Gospel's call to justice there is what theologian Paul Tillich called "a dimension of depth." Some of us have come to think of seeking and doing justice as our deepest experience of God, a connection often voiced by biblical prophets. Oh God can be like a coming home to God and to your truest and deepest self for others.

How, then, does the church go about the pursuit of justice? The quest best originates with questions like these:

1. Where is God leading and prompting us towards justice? Where is Jesus at work in our community or area on behalf of justice?

2. Is there any word from the Lord? This biblical question asked of Jeremiah by King Zedekiah (Jer. 37:17) breaks through our rational calculations and calls us to discernment and humility.

3. What injustice draws the strongest sense of passion and conviction from you or your group?

The composite question might be, "Where and how does our passion meet the needs of the community or world as prompted by the initiative of God through Jesus Christ?" And we had best take along for the ride a healthy practice of critical self-reflection in order to avoid self-righteousness. Then add a dose of humor to proceed on the wings of grace.

Any person or group or congregation on the path of doing justice will need to make strategic choices to address a particular issue. The possible strategies are many and the list suggested here is by no means exhaustive. Some of these will be examined in the context of actual efforts on behalf of justice, both in this chapter and in Chapter 5. All strategies given are intended to be nonviolent in both spirit and action.

Consider these nonviolent ways and means for justice work. They compose fertile discussion ground for preparing and evaluating action:

prayers	marches
letters and phone calls	sit-ins
petitions	legal action
silent vigils	civil disobedience
fasting	picketing
dialogue/persuasion	community organizing
newspaper ads	personal influence
lobbying	resolutions
justice-based social analysis	
educating church members and the public on political issues	

These strategies can be exercised in a variety of ways. Choices can include local church action, ecumenical or interfaith cooperation, and support of justice oriented organizations, programs and government agencies. Learning on the job to discern which of these strategies or combination thereof seems best in a particular situation is part of the ongoing challenge of the justice vocation. I have found it important to strive for a thoughtful blending of idealism and realism. When one overwhelms the other, naivete or despair is waiting to call your name.

Between Charity and Justice

The distinction between charity and justice is not always as clearly defined as we might think. Charitable efforts tend to meet a variety of human needs within a given system. Many congregations have a consistent and compassionate history in charitable work. Perhaps the most often used example is replenishing food banks and volunteering to dispense food to the hungry. Should justice oriented Christians who, let's face it, do not compose the whole church be critical of charitable efforts?

My reply is yes and no. No, if charity doers are supportive of others who take on justice seeking and doing. The plain fact is, whether we like it or not, there are many Christians able and willing to engage in charitable efforts but unable for a variety of reasons to take on the vocation of justice. This is on-the-ground realism. Another plain fact is that without charity, many people will starve to death while others of us are striving for a more just system. As Martin Luther King, Jr. suggested, justice is a marathon activity, not a simple sprint.

Our task is to keep on encouraging a greater number of Christians to seek and work for justice. This is gospel-supported idealism. I say to charity oriented Christians, "Try to see the larger task of justice and to understand the calling of the church to work for systemic change." A church that does not give itself to more humane systems is defective in its practice of the Gospel of Jesus Christ because love requires justice. Charity alone without striving for justice deserves to be questioned because it perpetuates the system partly responsible for hunger and other deficiencies of the present system. Years ago Archbishop Dom Helder Camara of Brazil said that when he encouraged feeding the poor, he was called a saint. When he asked why so many were hungry, he was called a communist.

Sometimes the church's ministry makes it possible for persons to achieve a much better life opportunity within the existing system. For example, let's say persons are empowered to find steady employment or to access better health care. Or perhaps they are assisted in locating and affording low cost housing. These improvements in quality of life are more than simple charity but somewhat less than justice because the overall system remains basically the same. Beyond charity yet less than justice ministries are often doable by congregations working as advocates with marginalized persons. Quality of life improvements can also encourage all concerned to better understand the present system and at the same time work for a more humane system.

The remainder of this chapter narrates six experiences in my ministry of seeking to do or support justice in a variety of settings. Nearly fifty years of ministry are represented. In each instance committed laity and clergy have shared the journey and have often been my mentors. My hope is that theological and practical reflections on each will shed light on strategies used, changes brought about, and thoughts from hindsight on how our efforts might have been more effective. I invite the reader to translate these stories into your present circumstances for edification and insight into justice seeking and the requisite strategies.

"Gentlemen, we'll see you in court."

Early in my ministry (1959) the bishop appointed me to a vacant lot. That's my way of saying I was to start a new congregation on the east side of Dallas in a suburban town called Mesquite. I knocked on about 1,700 doors in two weeks. The newly assembled congregation met in an elementary school and three years later completed a free form church building to house our congregation and its ministries. The congregation chose the name St. Stephen Methodist (now United Methodist) and settled in to be an expression of Christ's Body in this location.

One day a Presbyterian minister friend dropped by to visit. In the course of chitchat he posed the question, "Have you ever seen the Mesquite elementary school attended only by black children?" I replied that I had not and asked where the school was located. "Would you like to see it?" my friend asked. My curiosity and concern aroused, I said "Sure." Mesquite was a sprawling, mostly suburban community with much undeveloped land.

The school was situated off the suburban radar in an area still rural in location and appearance. Here's what we saw: a three-room schoolhouse with eight grades, no sidewalks, no playground equipment, no American flag. Injustice, I was to learn, is often accompanied by lack of visibility and virtual absence of transparency in the system. Meanwhile, doing our homework, we were to discover that the all-white Mesquite School District had managed to build a brand new science laboratory. There was more to learn. The black students of high school age living in Mesquite were shipped by bus to school in the nearby town of Forney. We took a look at that as well.

Our congregation had decisions to make. What do we do about this hidden and separate reality of the black school classes? How might we address the blatant discrimination? Will the Presbyterians get involved? Our first step was open discussion among our congregational leadership. This was not to be seen as a clergy issue but as a matter confronting the whole congregation. As I said to seminary students as a professor in later years, work with the laity, not above them, below them, or around them. Strategy number one is clergy and laity in serious discussion and reflection. We learn together, fail together, and succeed together. I saw it as my responsibility to offer biblical and theological connections and in particular, to the inseparability of the theological and the political. Our discussion was about the prophetic ministry of the congregation that belongs to the whole church and finally, to Jesus Christ. There was not unanimity but there was consensus that we could not be in denial and stick our head in some otherworldly piety. We had to do something.

That initial something was to make contact with the black parents. It took some effort just to locate them, as they were few yet scattered in different locations within Mesquite. We needed to know what the parents thought about the schooling of their children. Perhaps they would think it best to leave it alone. After all they, along with the black teachers, were the most vulnerable. St. Stephen would not pursue an integrated system without permission of the black families. I should say here that the Presbyterian congregation had a plate full of other challenges, so it was up to St. Stephen to carry on.

The upshot of contact with the black families was their choice not to be directly involved but with assurance they would support us in our attempt to bring about a more just system of education. "What do we have to lose?" was their fundamental attitude. At this point there was no agreement as to what long range strategy might be forthcoming since we were not sure ourselves.

Before proceeding on our own, our immediate plan was to search for a black church in Mesquite. In hindsight we would have done better to begin there so that all concerned parties could start on the ground floor. Remember, I was pretty green at the justice vocation and so were our church members for the most part. To our surprise we were unable to locate the presence of a black congregation within Mesquite. Maybe there was invisibility here, too, as with the black school. Maybe we were not sufficiently diligent in these attempts. If we had this to do over our church would have sought the counsel of black leadership beyond Mesquite since none seemed available within. The Civil Rights movement was to teach us greater justice discernment and skills.

Our next strategy was to arrange a meeting with the Mesquite School Board. We eschewed writing letters or petitions in favor of direct face-to-face contact. Two of our laity, one being an attorney, and I secured an appointment with the school board. We decided in advance we would express our concerns resulting from our previous research and contacts. Then we would listen to sense the response of the board members. The atmosphere was cordial yet cool, both parties respectful of the other. The board would take our concerns under consideration.

Time passed. No word forthcoming. We initiated a second meeting, hoping to go more deeply into the matter. Our strategy was to offer a conciliatory method of communication. Theologian and social critic Reinhold Niebuhr used to say that justice seekers owe it to those in power to first try moral persuasion, but that it seldom works. Entrenched systems favorable to the powerful rarely become the way they are by accident or simple carelessness. The meeting ended without any agreements or indications of change. Again time passed. We took silence from the board to mean that they probably thought we would tire of these efforts and simply go away. It wasn't going to happen. By this time our resolve was stronger than ever.

With some difficulty and resistance from the board, a third session was arranged. There was no sign of progress or even consideration of serious future conversation. Our frustration and disappointment grew during the meeting. We found ourselves moving emotionally and psychologically from a conciliatory stance to a more confrontational one. As our St. Stephen group of three left the room, these words unexpectedly came out of my mouth: "Gentlemen, we'll see you in court (they were all male). You are in violation of the United States Constitution (more accurately existing Civil Rights Laws). The treatment of black students and teachers is immoral and a disgrace to our community."

On the way back to the church the two St. Stephen members understandably registered their shock and surprise at my statement of legal action. "Where did that come from?" they inquired. I had to admit I wasn't really sure. I knew any attempt to blame it on the Holy Spirit would be futile. At any rate we decided to see what would come to pass. I'm not sure where the funds for legal action would have come from, but to this day I'm convinced we would have somehow raised them.

Maybe the Holy Spirit was at work after all. Within forty-eight hours I received a phone call from the school board chairman. "Let's talk," he suggested. I of course accepted his offer. Though tardy and reluctant, responding only after threat of legal action, credit should be given to the school board for initiating and implementing a plan of integration. In a two- year process equal educational opportunity was provided for black students and teachers.

All of this did not take place without risk. St. Stephen lost a few members who thought we were political instead of religious, as though the two could be separated in this situation. The black parents were courageous in being willing to risk further humiliation in the hope of being treated as first class citizens. The school board members were not evil men. They were decent persons caught in a system that expected them to observe cultural conditions in place all of their lives. They risked criticism from fellow citizens and church colleagues for embracing a new future. In subsequent years a new high school in Mesquite was named for the school board chair. And why not? Progress was made.

A common definition of insanity is doing the same thing over and over again and expecting to get a different result. This is a half-truth at best. Remember the never-give-up widow who kept bugging the judge in Luke 18? She kept coming until the judge in exasperation granted her wish for vindication, exclaiming, "She will wear me out by her continual coming." Although new approaches are to be considered, the widow's persistence is often the way of justice seekers.

This narrative tells of my first real participation in seeking justice as pastor of a congregation. We probably could have, maybe should have, chosen other nonviolent strategies, such as letters, public vigils, or one on one visits with school board members. In spite of whatever mistakes we may have made, St. Stephen grew in the conviction that justice is basic to the congregation's life and what it means to follow in the footsteps of Jesus. To this day I give thanks for the faithful witness of St. Stephen laity.

Custodians and Secretaries Included

When people who are affected by institutional decisions are not offered the right to influence those decisions or at least be heard, the guaranteed result is resentment and resistance. In more than fifty years of organizational experience, both religious and secular, I have seldom seen an exception. The negative response may be silently passive-aggressive or take the form of a more public confrontation.

Not long after I came to Saint Paul School of Theology as president in 1973, concerns regarding the governance structure of the seminary began to surface. The seminary had already developed a remarkable sense of community, but the organization on the ground did not reflect adequately that reality.

So we began to put some heads together. The faculty and the students had their own councils. As a freestanding (not university related) seminary, the trustees had their appropriate authority as provided by the seminary by-laws. The alumni/ae had representation on the board of trustees. Where was the staff represented?

Most seminaries, as well as other educational institutions, would grind to a very slow pace without secretaries, maintenance personnel, and other staff personnel. The work of the faculty and administration would be seriously hampered and thus students would also be negatively affected. The condition of campus building and grounds would be in serious jeopardy. It's not unusual for the secretaries and maintenance crews to receive the least credit and yet perform the most tedious or strenuous work.

Time for action was apparent. Through a process of negotiation and preparation the governance structure was altered to add a staff council with the staff's consent and encouragement. The staff council elected its own chair and was represented for the first time on the seminary's board of trustees. Not the least benefit of the process was educating the whole seminary on power issues that are inevitably justice related concerns.

There are several other aspects of the more inclusive governance to note. The work of the staff became credited on a visible, ongoing basis. The community life was deepened through a stronger sense of justice and respect for staff. In this case, since all the secretaries were female and the maintenance staff blue-collar male, the larger circle of inclusion addressed gender and class in an indirect manner. Theologically the change set an example not only on the campus but also for future pastors in their churches and for seeking justice in a society of great disparities in the work place. The Social Principles of the United Methodist Church uphold humane working conditions and support for a living wage.

Do you have any openings?

During the Civil Rights movement in the 1960s I was active in the Neighbors for Fair Housing organization. We employed several strategies designed to ensure the practice of justice in housing availability. Our foremost strategy was to send a black couple to inquire about renting an apartment. If the owners or their representative said to the black couple that the space was not available, Neighbors would shortly thereafter commission a white couple to apply. All who agreed to test the market in this way were carefully trained to interpret both verbal and visual signs, to not react negatively while applying, and to report accurately on returning to Neighbors headquarters or base of operation in a given neighborhood.

Critics complained about lack of sincerity on the part of inquirers trained by Neighbors since there was no intent to occupy even if space were available. Our response was how else could fair housing be determined. Not only that but what about the lack of integrity on the part of racist apartment owners? If it were not for that injustice there would be no need for testing. When discrepancy in practice was clearly evident, the owner was given the chance to make it right and to change the system on a permanent basis. Refusal to do so could lead to litigation and the negative publicity that would come with legal action.

I include this justice example on behalf of fair housing for several reasons. It calls attention to an action in which individual church members could participate at the time. Sometimes a congregation initiates its own program or plan serving justice on a chosen issue. At other times church members sign up to work in an already existing organization working for justice such as Neighbors for Fair Housing. Neighbors had a strong Jewish presence, bringing together Jews and Christians working for *tikkun olam*, that is, repairing the world and reshaping it in the form of justice. Look around and see what God is doing through ecumenical, interfaith, and so-called secular organizations in your city, town, or county.

Another strategy we utilized was the use of newspaper ads to foster transparency of information and awareness. An ad in a Dallas newspaper urged passage of fair housing legislation pending in Congress and warned against being misled by the "scare psychology of realtors who wished to profit from Un-American discrimination." One strategy question to ponder is whether the appeal, in whatever form, is made from a patriotic position or from a clearly stated faith basis. Or both.

Love turns fear into joy

Ten years ago thirty members of Northaven United Methodist Church in Dallas gathered in the home of a church member. We had gathered a number of times previously. Somehow I still think of this particular evening as the occasion in which Northaven turned a corner in our quest to become a truly open and welcoming congregation. Others may remember it differently or recall some other event as Northaven's Damascus road/Aldersgate experience.

More than ever before those of us who are straight or heterosexual heard story after story of pain and rejection from our lesbian and gay friends. Sometimes the hurt was imposed by family. One member told of his family returning his Christmas gifts; another was denied parental hospitality unless she was willing to end a relationship with a same sex partner. Stories of being humiliated by the church were all too frequent. "You are not welcome to join here; you are an abomination; unless you repent and change your life style you will end up in hell." Employment sometimes hinged on either pretending to be heterosexual or closely hiding sexual identity. I will not forget the sorrow, the burden shared, or the need for acceptance made so clear that evening.

For years I have believed some of us who are straight come to the vocation of justice because we have heard and felt the lamentation and pain of others who have become our friends. Many Christians are reasonably open to hearing the injustices experienced by others, especially when a human face or association takes the place of a previous stereotype. Rational thought has its place in overcoming our blind spots, but most of us change because of relationships and the discovery of mutual vulnerability. We may be tempted to see those who have been hurt solely as victims. We do better to see ourselves as learners in need of mentors who can teach us the ABC's of social reality. We need each other to be whole.

Northaven wrestled for nine years before making a deliberate decision to become a reconciling congregation, an unofficial self-designation used by some United Methodist congregations. There are also campus ministries and adult classes that use the term. We entered into extended bible study, dialogue, and invited other United Methodists who were going in a similar direction to come and share their minds and hearts.

During our lengthy process of study and discernment one of my dearest straight friends at Northaven fretted about the possibility of becoming "a gay church." Others feared "being overrun" by GLBT persons (gay, lesbian, bi-sexual, transgender). My response was that we don't have to be concerned with quotas or percentages. Just be the church, welcome all who come, and leave the rest to God. So it has been. On one occasion when all the adult classes were gathered for conversation about our congregation's future, one member declared,

"This church has saved me from my homophobia." Immediately another member said, "Yes, and this church has saved me from my heterophobia!" It works both ways. Our straight members have learned that many GLBT's have never been loved for who they are by straight persons. I can't think of a better way for the church to follow in the footsteps of Jesus, the advocate for the marginalized. Although I don't take credit for it, I'm profoundly grateful to have served as pastor of two congregations in the North Texas Conference of The United Methodist Church that became reconciling congregations.

Personal Theological Reflections

During my pastorates years ago I was deeply challenged by the Civil Rights movement in the 1960's. In the 1970's I was impacted by the feminist movement. About the same time third world liberation theology altered my thinking, especially about doing justice. Then appeared theology and call for changes from those with disabilities (some prefer differently-abled or other terms). All of these winds of theological change became my mentors through hearing lectures, reading books, meeting people, and travel to other cultures. My theology of sexuality, especially in regard to homosexuality and gay rights, was less developed than theology represented in the other movements mentioned above. I am tremendously indebted to personal friendships with gays and lesbians through whom Northaven became the primary agent of new understanding and awareness.

One of my favorite authors is Elizabeth Dodson Gray. She uses the term "conceptual trap" to talk about where we are and need to go as persons and as the church. She says a conceptual trap is like being born into a room with no windows. Reality has already been named. It's always been this way, always will be. Just get used to it. She says the task of the church is to break through these conceptual traps, to create alternatives and alterations. Just one example will suffice.

When I was a seminary student in the 1950's the few female students were training for positions in Christian education. The church was in a conceptual trap in which women were not ordained. Today women make up from one-third to one-half or more of seminary students in United Methodist seminaries as well as in many other denominations. While the church is in dire need of Christian educators, the majority of women seminary students have the local church pastorate in mind. In 1956 the Methodist Church voted to grant full clergy rights to women. How many other conceptual traps have been broken or at least challenged in the past several decades up to our present time. The church continues to struggle in a conceptual trap that limits the gifts of gay and lesbian members or would-be members.

Over a period of time I have become convinced that scripture does not define our identity by race, gender, class, sexual orientation, or any other human circumstance or vicissitude. These are important features of our lives but they are not determinate of our identity in God. Scripture defines our identity theologically by *imago dei*, by our being born in the image of God. Scripture begins here (Genesis 1:27). There are no exceptions. Our worth as human beings should not be open to votes cast by either church or society.

Scripture defines our identity liturgically, in the case of Christians, by baptism. Baptism proclaims and visibly enacts God's gift of unconditional love. The faith community responds by making covenant to nourish and love the baptized in faith, hope, and love. The liturgy provides no exception, as though the commitment of the congregation can be cancelled if the baptized, whether child, youth, or adult, turns out to be lesbian or gay.

Scripture defines our identity morally, ethically, behaviorally by the Great Commandment: Love God with heart, soul, mind, and strength, and neighbor as yourself ... and of course there is not a shred of evidence that GLBT's are any less able or willing to fulfill God's Will as expressed in the Great Commandment than heterosexuals.

How can Christians miss the comprehensive "magnetic field" of New Testament texts bearing God's unconditional love expressed through word and deed by Jesus Christ? These are pervasive and found in all the gospels. Particularly striking is Jesus' friendship and affirmation of those rejected or dismissed by the religion or culture around him. How can these plentiful texts be less important to Christians than a Pauline text and one or two others that show no knowledge of long term same sex adult consensual relationships? Paul's understanding of homosexuality in the ancient world is no more relevant to today's gay rights than food laws in Leviticus are binding for today's generation of Christians and those to come.

Since the scripture is so often used to justify exclusion of GLBT's, I want to emphasize again what I believe to be true biblical authority. The church should be concerned with being biblical in the deepest sense. The ranking of a few questionable statements by Paul above all the pervasive and powerful texts related to God's radical love in Jesus can hardly qualify as serious biblical inquiry and authority. To be profoundly biblical from a Christian standpoint is to give prominence and priority to what Jesus lifted up as discipleship and authentic life in response to God's love.

In more than fifty years of ministry as a pastor, seminary administrator and professor in the United Methodist Church, counting my active and "retired" years, I have been privileged to know talented and dedicated gay and lesbian theological students eager to serve in our denomination. Many of them have been life long United Methodists, baptized and raised in our churches. Yet, unless silent and secretive about loving relationships, they have been denied ordination, excluded in the name of God as being defective and unworthy. Automatically barring gay men and lesbians from ordination because they "love the wrong neighbor" is an offense to the gospel of God's love expressed through Jesus Christ.

If truth were known, homosexuals have been practicing ordained ministry in our church and in others since the beginning of ordination. The stumbling block is not in their ability to practice ministry faithfully and effectively, but in the blindness of the heterosexual community to recognize and credit God-given gifts, call, and commitment. "Don't ask, don't tell" has been the functioning principle of a fearful church. There is no evidence that gays and lesbians are less capable than straights in service, word, sacrament, and order, or in conviction and confidence in God's call to ordained ministry.

By rejecting qualified lesbians and gays for ordination, the church unwittingly yet inevitably colludes with a society too often bent on individual and collective violence toward homosexuals. When the church gives signals that GLBT's are a threat to the church, we tacitly approve anti-gay action incompatible with the Christian gospel of love. I believe there will be rejoicing in heaven when the church truly opens doors, minds, and hearts without reservation to all of God's people.

More on Northaven's Journey

I have written at length on Northaven's experience because without doubt it has been one of the most freeing and growth-filled ventures in the congregation's more than fifty years. Much credit belongs to a laity with both gays and straights willing to take risks, to the ministry of hospitality encouraged by pastor DeForrest Wiksten, the prophetic leadership of pastors Bourdon Smith and John Thornburg, and sustained and enabled by pastor Eric Folkerth. Our congregation is richer in community, in our understanding and experience of God's love, and in talent and total resources. We haven't gone on to perfection in love, as John Wesley might say, but we rejoice in God's gift of inclusive community. We are told by other congregations and their leaders that we set an example for others to consider.

We took plenty of time for everyone to be heard and to process feelings and fears. For those interested I would say that something like one-third of our members are gays and lesbians. Endless meetings took place and bible study undergirded it all. New members, both gay and straight, come partly because they want to be part of a prejudice free church environment centered in love and acceptance.

It's all about love and discovery of joy that overcomes fear based on stereotypes and outdated knowledge. I find myself wanting to say to fearful Christians, "If you would just give it a try, God will walk with you on the path of new friendship and advocacy for human rights as you discover the fullness of Jesus' love." Justice for GLBT's is the outgrowth of this love. Once you discover the freedom of friendship you are not likely to return to former ways.

Here are strategies to consider in moving toward becoming a welcoming, justice seeking congregation:

1. Center on Jesus' life and example. Follow in his footsteps as barrier breaker, community maker. In other words, concentrate on God's radical love. Remember, Paul is important but Paul is not Lord.

2. Encourage open conversation so that people do not feel left out or ignored. Don't look for a cakewalk, but do look for signs of a Divine love from which comes courage and willingness to listen and share experiences

3. Practice hospitality and discern the leading of the Holy Spirit. Open doors, minds, and hearts can transform a community.

4. Talk with members of a reconciling congregation to hear their stories. While each situation is different, they can serve as guides and supporters.

5. Consider bible study focusing on Jesus' parables and example. What seem to be the common denominators? What do they suggest for today's church?

6. Make friends across the lines of sexual identity. Doing so between whites and racial minorities has opened minds and hearts over the years. Let "the other" into your life for mutual learning and support. Remember, every friend we now have was once a total stranger.

In a lecture at Southern Methodist University, Rev. Joseph Lowery, former head of the Southern Christian Leadership Conference, told this story. During the Civil Rights movement he was living in Memphis. He made it a point to visit a nearby restaurant each week to test the segregated system. On his first attempt to be served, he ordered a hamburger. The white waitress replied, "We don't serve Negroes." Rev. Lowery replied, "I didn't ask to be served a Negro. I asked to be served a hamburger." He did not get his hamburger. Each week he returned and ordered a hamburger from the same waitress with the same result.

Finally, as the Civil Rights movement took root across the South, the mayor of Memphis declared all retail establishments would be desegregated. So Rev. Lowery returned and ordered his hamburger. The waitress replied, "How would you like it prepared?" He replied, "Well done." When the waitress brought the hamburger, she said, "Would you let me pay for it?" Rev. Lowery thanked her but insisted on paying for his long awaited treat. He then told his lecture audience, "Do you realize what the waitress was saying to me? She was exclaiming the thought of Martin Luther King, Jr. in his *I Have a Dream* speech, 'Thank God Almighty, free at last, free at last.'"

Our conceptual traps imprison oppressor and oppressed alike. I believe there are countless persons in our churches who deep down want to be free at last from fear and free for the blessed community of God's love but who are weighed down by stereotypes, fear of the unknown, peer pressure, and the need to conform. I believe there are others who don't know yet that they want to be free at last but who, in

God's grace, may come to that freedom in due time. It's all about love and joy, not fear.

Praying with Our Feet

The late Abraham Joshua Heschel, at one time Professor of Ethics and Mysticism at Jewish Theological Seminary in New York, spoke of praying with his feet. He was an active participant in the Civil Rights movement and in calling for peace through protests against the Vietnam War.

In the many marches in which I have participated I have sought to be part of public witness for the cause of justice. A short list includes peace marches in Dallas and Washington D.C. calling for peace in Vietnam; a march in Washington D.C. commemorating the tenth anniversary of Archbishop Oscar Romero's assassination; a march in the nation's capitol remembering the tenth anniversary of Martin Luther King's *I Have a Dream* address; co-leading a march and rally in Dallas supporting the Poor People's Campaign; a number of marches either urging our government not to go to war in Iraq or calling for an end to the war; a march and rally at Fort Benning, Georgia calling for the closure of the School of the Americas; a Holy Week procession lifting up Jesus' values for our world described in Matthew 25.

Each of the marches was focused around one or more issues of peace and justice. The anti-war marches frequently mirrored the call by Martin Luther King, Jr. for challenging militarism, poverty, and racism. The Poor People's Campaign sought a place at the legislative table in Washington for those without a public voice. Many marches were an attempt to address U.S. foreign policy in Latin America, Vietnam, Iraq, or in a wider area. Speakers and banners addressed these themes verbally and visually.

Sponsors vary from peace organizations, ecumenical groups, and civil rights organizations. It's not unusual to have joint sponsorship by several groups striving to meet similar goals. Sometimes groups gather at a designated location rather than take on an extended march.

What good do marches do?

People frequently ask, "Do marches really do any good? Do they result in the desired changes of those who march and those who speak? Do they alter public policy or even the values of individuals?" I believe marches can serve at least three purposes.

1. To strengthen the resolve of those who walk for the intended cause. This is akin to preaching to the choir yet is not to be easily dismissed. Marchers usually, though not always, represent a minority position that may be highly unpopular in the broader society. Accusations of being troublemakers, unpatriotic, or un-American are not rare. It's good to have company on controversial matters.

2. To be in solidarity and support of people yearning for justice. Marching with African Americans, Latinos/as, GLBT persons, and immigrants makes the learning process of advocacy public and offers encouragement to marginalized groups. These experiences can be among the best in learning the nuts and bolts of justice issues from those who know best.

3. To influence public opinion and public policy. Every act of courage and accompaniment on behalf of justice emboldens others to either change their positions towards greater enlightenment or to hold fast to an unpopular stand already taken. And while the mills of Congress tend to grind slowly, they are not immune from public expression of protest and challenge. American history is full of change brought from grass roots marches, rallies, and vigils for voting rights, an end to war, and equal access.

How well a march serves its particular purpose cannot be predicted in advance or defined immediately afterwards. Matters of faith and societal change are not easily calibrated into provable facts. Frequently it is only in looking back in hindsight that insight becomes more apparent.

Some of the factors influencing results are the national ethos in which the event takes place, the advance publicity and coverage by print and electronic media, how well the event is organized, the quality of the speakers and their message, and the faithfulness of participants to the principles of nonviolence in their behavior.

Strategic Questions to Consider

1. Who is sponsoring and organizing the event? This is not always easy to determine to the fullest, but you many get some clues. You may want to make a contact or two to get a sense of what to expect. In spite of careful preparation by you and those organizing the march, there is no guarantee that all will go as planned. Don't expect perfection or agreement with everything said or done. Stay focused on the cause and on the many things that will go as expected and imagined.

2. What is the issue at stake which a proposed march or vigil wishes to address? Do you have a conviction or growing concern compatible with the stated goal of the march? Being in a rally is a good way to go public with other like-minded citizens. Some rallies prepare participants to consider nonviolent civil disobedience. Each marcher must decide for oneself. What might be most effective? Where does one's conscience lead? What are the consequences legally, financially, and even health-wise?

I have never regretted participating in any of the many opportunities to "pray with my feet." Virtually without exception there have been inspiring speakers, including Martin Luther King, Jr., Rabbi Heschel, and William Sloane Coffin in Washington D.C. marches. In Dallas area events I have been edified by many capable speakers and upon occasion have assumed the task of speaking. As I reflect through the years, I can say with joy and gratitude that walking for peace and justice has inspired my faith, lifted my hope, strengthened friendships, and challenged the public and our government to rethink the direction of our nation and its policies and practices.

Sometimes there are completely unexpected surprises. Once in a Washington D.C. rally against the Vietnam War, a sizable group of us marched from the Lincoln Memorial across the bridge to Arlington National Cemetery. We were led by Rev. King and Rabbi Heschel. As we entered the grounds, some cemetery workers were sitting on the curb having their sack lunches. Facing us was a group led by Carl McIntire, a well-known Communist baiter of the time. During this face-off of the two groups the cemetery chapel bells were pealing out *What a Friend We Have in Jesus*! What ever happened to the separation of church and state? As you can imagine, the workers, like the rest of us, were completely befuddled at this weird scene. At any rate we were able to proceed without undue interruption to complete our march in the appropriate cemetery setting.

On another occasion a sizable group of peace marchers had gathered at a square in downtown Dallas. We were protesting the Ballistic Missile system being considered by our government. Three of us, Protestant, Catholic, and Jewish, served as brief preliminary speakers. As we spoke members of the American Nazi party circled the square. Our keynote speaker was a retired military general. He was well into his message when a man bolted out of the crowd yelling, "Hitler was right" and threw red paint on the general and on two of us standing nearby. The attacker was immediately tackled by one of our group and hauled off in a paddy wagon by the police. We offered handkerchiefs to the general. Like a military officer going back to his post and continuing his mission, the general proceeded to finish his presentation. Fortunately the paint was water based and thus not too difficult to remove later from our faces and clothing. As my friend Richard Deats exclaimed, "Better red than dead!" If you pray with your feet do so with gumption, gravitas, and gratitude.

Learning from *Campesinos*

Effective efforts to secure justice usually begin with listening and learning. Victims of injustice know the most about the daily specifics of their oppression and what remedies might be most possible. To be in solidarity with marginalized people requires going back to school. The indigenous will be the professors and mentors. Those of us who seek to walk with them towards the light of justice will be the students. This is to say, then, that victims of systemic oppression, whatever form it may take in a given situation, are more than victims.

As I write this I'm thinking of a 1988 experience in a rural area not far from Matagalpa, Nicaragua. Our group from the United States was sitting on rustic benches in a one-room schoolhouse. We were taking notes from a presentation given by *campesinos* who were the local agrarian land experts. This is a frequent narrative of justice seeking.

On the same excursion to Central America, our group of about fourteen clergy and laity had the opportunity to travel some distance from the Salvadoran capitol of San Salvador to the rural community of

Santa Marta. Most of the people of Santa Marta had recently returned from the Mesa Grande refugee camp across the Honduran border. They showed us the remains of their chapel destroyed by the Salvadoran Air Force during the civil war still being waged. Weeds had grown over where the Eucharistic table had been located. Now they were building new houses and starting life over again. They welcomed us as friends and shared a meal from meager resources.

New houses of wood and corrugated tin roofing were in process of being built and completed on the other side of the river from where most of the people had temporarily relocated. Several realities dawned on our visiting group from the United States. First was the jolt to our U.S.-formed culture of individualized thinking. The Santa Marta community had made a group decision: no one would move across the river into the newly developed housing until all could move together. Not exactly our suburban life style!

A second awareness was the radical nature of their hospitality. They seemed to have no difficulty in welcoming and trusting us although we were *norteamericanos* whose government was supporting the Salvadoran hierarchy and military. Somehow their faith and wisdom enabled them to distinguish between U.S. citizens who had come among them and the U.S. government policies and practices contributing to their loss and misery.

A third memorable realization on our part was that the Santa Marta community was completely vulnerable to further attacks and humiliations by the Salvadoran military. The armed forces could return at will and destroy all the new houses and even the people themselves, especially the leaders. The slightest indication of subversive activity by any member of the community could and probably would result in the whole community being subjected to harassment.

The Leaders Council, speaking through an interpreter, spent time with us explaining their circumstances and receiving our questions. One of our questions was, "Given the complete vulnerability in which you live, where is your hope?" I expect none of our group will ever forget the reply. They described a twofold hope for their future, one religious and one political, yet each inseparable from the other. "Our hope is in the crucified, risen Lord." When they elaborated on the theological hope, it sounded like this: "Jesus was poor, broken and despised like us.

He was a victim of violence like us, but resisted injustice to the point of death. He is one of us. Who else would die for us? His risen victory over all his oppressors gives us courage to carry on." Jesus' death on the cross was like a seal and sign of solidarity with Santa Marta. It was an unbreakable bond.

To this day the Santa Marta *campesinos'* trust in the saving power of Jesus' crucifixion and resurrection remains more memorable and uplifting to me than all the atonement theories espoused by professional or academic theologians, both past and present.

Secondly, their hope was in our urging our leaders in the United States to cease supporting the Salvadoran military and death squads. So we were given our marching orders if we were going to be in solidarity with Santa Marta. We had to be their voice in high places in our own country, speaking truth to power back home. Ever since this event I have been tested by the *campesinos'* courage, their clarity as to how theological and political reality merges into one hope, and their bringing together a pastoral hospitality for us combined with a claim on our faith as Christians to make their concern our own.

Accordingly, we came home speaking a newly learned truth to various levels of power. What strategies could we utilize? We wrote letters and made calls to our congressional representatives. Those of us from the Dallas area contacted local news media with some success in terms of their reporting our stories from Santa Marta. We spoke out in our churches, not only about facts on the ground in Santa Marta, but also concerning U.S. policy in Latin America, both past and present. In Chapter 5 an ongoing justice journey with Maria Madre de los Pobres parish in San Salvador will be offered.

Important justice lessons reside in these experiences. Clarity of successful results is often not given to us. This can be discouraging to those who require a definitive outcome. We seek to be effective in justice vocation but we need to trust the Holy Spirit for results we may never know, yet travel that fine line of not using the Spirit as an excuse for less than our best efforts. We easily convince ourselves that our little part of the big picture is so small it's hardly worth the effort. From a faith standpoint it is precisely our "little part" that largely defines the meaning of our lives and our faithfulness to the Gospel. Jesus gives no worldly guarantee of victory other than the victory of living for risk-filled truth itself.

Questions for reflection and discussion

1. What justice issue(s) would you like for your congregation to address?

2. How is your congregation responding to the biblical mandate "to do justice, love mercy, and walk humbly with God" (Micah 6)?

3. Thinking back over your years in the church, what justice issues have been engaged by the local church, or by regional and national bodies of your denomination? What strategies were used?

4. From whom do we need to learn?

5. If doing justice through your congregation has resulted in conflict, how has this been addressed? Could different strategies have been used?

CHAPTER 5

THE COMPANY OF PROPHETS TODAY

Every prophet is a mystery in which God uses a human being to reveal what we need right now.

Megan McKenna

The prophets were completely committed to the truth. They were totally opposed to exploitation and demanded justice for the poor. They opposed all empires and believed empires had no future.

Philip Wheaton

The eleven narratives composing this chapter speak to issues of economic justice, human rights, immigration, environment, peace and justice through the coming together of Muslims and Christians, international justice, and community violence. These real life stories are written by both clergy and laity in small and large congregations and are titled by the authors. Some of the narratives reflect on justice experiences some years ago while others are in current process. I believe each story, whether past or present, invites reflection and action pertinent for today's vocation of justice.

These examples of what's going on "out there" suggest the validity of the chapter's subtitle, "the road more traveled." In the process of the book's development I discovered that the seeking and doing of justice in Christian congregations is more widespread than I originally imagined.

The narratives in this chapter come mostly from the relatively small circle of my own contacts and connections. I am indebted to the authors who took the time and the leap of faith to join in lifting up examples of their efforts to do justice, love mercy, and walk humbly with God. Perhaps their willingness to participate in a larger manuscript over which they had no control or even much information indicates the risk-taking nature of putting oneself on the line for justice.

I am under no illusion, however, that there can be easy comparison of these stories of justice vocation with the biblical prophets. Connecting biblical prophets to the changing society in which we live is at best problematical. Whatever prior connection they had with Israelite tradition, the biblical prophets seem to come out of nowhere in the sense that they just appear and utter the word of the Lord. They are un-credentialed by any worldly organization or agency. As indicated in this book's opening paragraphs, they did not function in the religious world of budgets, buildings, and organizational expectations. The prophets uttered God's judgment and promise of restoration rather than being social activists as we might think of today's justice seekers and doers. Yet for our time the efforts related in this chapter, warts and all, represent the biblical prophetic spirit and provide examples of justice vocation to be considered, critically evaluated and, if desired, emulated. They offer theological grounding and strategic choices and, in my opinion, represent integrity of engagement and depth of insight and discernment. I have insisted that each writer have complete freedom in the content and writing style of his or her story. Editing for clarity or brevity has been minimal.

I invite each reader to become the twelfth contributor of justice seeking and doing by making known to others your own justice vocation, past or present.

Pastors-for-Peace: Dismantling Borders with Love and Justice
By Diane Baker

I begin this writing with a spirit graced by the Holy Spirit, the spirit of a just God blowing through a very fragile world, congregations and individuals who have been touched by the ministry of a program called

IFCO/P4P. This program has been the fruit of a vision begun by a man who has the bright smile of a young child, the wisdom of a very old man, the strength and creative energy of a youth, and the spirit of one called by God to be with God's people. Knowing the blessings of working with Pastors for Peace, it made sense to me that I should involve my own congregation, other congregations and the greater community. The message of Pastors, like the message of the gospel, is radical. I believe we have been called to be a radical people of God.

IFCO, the Interreligious Foundation for Community Organization, was founded in 1967 by progressive church leaders and activists, led by the Rev. Lucius Walker, a Baptist minister. For over 40 years IFCO's mission has been to advance the cause of oppressed people struggling for justice and self-determination and to assist them in developing and sustaining community organizations to oppose human and civil rights injustices.

In 1988 Rev. Walker was in Central America on a fact-finding trip. On a ferry in Nicaragua, his group was attacked by paramilitary forces known as Contras. Rev. Walker, along with 31 others, was shot. As he recovered in the hospital, he realized that his own government had paid for the bullets that almost killed him. As a man of faith he decided to use his resources to pursue peace and reconciliation. He organized a program to deliver aid to our neighbors to the south and learn better how to help them. He called this program Pastors-for-Peace.

Pastors-for-Peace was created as a special ministry of IFCO to pioneer the delivery of humanitarian aid to Latin America and the Caribbean. Since 1988 thousands of people have participated in Pastors-for-Peace caravans to Mexico, Central America, and Cuba and in many other delegations and work brigades. The caravans to Cuba, known as "Friendshipments," have served as powerful challenges to the immorality and illegality of our government's cruel economic blockade and travel ban of Cuba. Over the years the Pastors caravans have delivered more than 2,000 tons of aid to Cuba without requesting a license from the U.S. government. It is the view of IFCO that the church and its outreach branches need not ask the government for permission to do the Lord's work.

Here is how it works: Every few months, volunteers from across the country create a caravan of old school buses and trucks. The caravan is supported by donations to IFCO/Pastors-for-Peace. The volunteers include people of all interests: students, clergy, laity, people of all manner of faith and belief, social workers, doctors, teachers, retirees, pastors, but always a good mechanic who is required on each trip to keep the old buses running when they break down in the middle of the Central American jungle. The caravan originates with groups all across the country, where Pastors supporters buy old school buses and begin the journey southward. The various parts of the caravan drive across the United States, stopping in many cities where the "*caravanistas*" meet with churches and civic groups who have collected medicine, school supplies, building materials and food. The caravans eventually make their way to places such as Mexico, El Salvador, Honduras, Nicaragua and Cuba, where the material is distributed to prearranged places.

In 1995 I received my immersion into Pastors by going with a caravan to Nicaragua. Hurricane Mitch had just devastated much of Central America. Pictures of the faces of victims of that tragedy prompted me to make a last-minute decision to go with the Pastors relief caravan.

I was able to travel with Pastors when El Salvador was still reeling with widespread political violence. The warfare was often focused on "soft targets," such as when Archbishop Romero and, later, six Jesuits and their housekeeper and daughter were murdered. During this time, "death squads" caused the murder or disappearance of tens of thousands, creating the refugee camps as the population tried to flee from the terror. This experience plunged me into the depths of sorrow for my own country's involvement in this terrible situation. In spite of this knowledge, we put the resources we had – our presence, companionship, and some material aid – to use in positive ways, instead of the purchasing of guns and bullets. We cannot separate the scriptural call to be people of justice from the call to help people satisfy their basic needs. We tried to be there to represent all who would extend a hand of compassion and that cool drink of water.

In 2001 I was one of twelve Americans who participated in the tenth caravan to Chiapas. The experience was draining, both physically and emotionally, because I saw more clearly how the indigenous people's lives have been affected by the unrelenting pressure of the paramilitaries who serve the interests of a few landholders.

On our first day in Chiapas we trekked over hills on dirt roads to a small resettling community of the indigenous. We traveled two hours by bus on a winding dirt road. When our bus broke down, we hiked the final miles to reach the mountain community. Upon arriving, we were told to wait outside the town while the local council decided whether we could stay. I couldn't believe it – after all, we had come all this way with things they needed.

Within an hour the council of leaders for the indigenous tribe decided to allow us to stay. They greeted us with music and dancing. After working, eating and sleeping with the people in primitive circumstances, I began to understand. History had taught them fear of strangers. Pride had taught them to set boundaries. Love had taught them gentleness and the blessing of dignity. I sensed that in being with them, I was changing because I had been blessed and was standing on sacred ground.

We visited churches, government and civic offices to listen to their understanding of the situation and to ask questions about the problems facing the indigenous peoples. We helped with construction work for a church and a children's clinic. Eventually, we delivered all eleven tons of goods that we brought, mostly to places where refugees are attempting resettlement. In a Chiapas village called Acteal I was invited to participate in a ceremony commemorating the fourth anniversary of a massacre. Forty-five people — mostly women and children – had been herded into a small church and shot to death by "paramilitary" forces that oppose the settlements of the indigenous people.

Justice and reconciliation seem unlikely in Chiapas. The government has released a number of the government-backed paramilitary who took part in the massacre. Meanwhile, we remain concerned for the survival of many people who were displaced by military force. When these indigenous people return to their communities, they have dwindling means of survival because their lands and crops were destroyed. Their struggles appear to have increased. Each day I was reminded of the similar persecution of Native Americans. Daily I was reminded of the sacred ground on which I stood.

Chiapas is rich with natural resources. And yet half the people have no potable water. Two-thirds have no sewage services. One and a half million get no medical services. Nearly half the babies die. Poverty has forced most of the children to work. They worked hard, cooking, washing clothes, and carrying heavy loads of corn and wood. Daily I was blessed by being in the presence of these children of God.

I have new respect and love for these people. I am humbled by their creative and gentle energy, and I share their hope to build a better world. As I write this, I find myself in conflict. I have the luxury of resting and reflecting, and I have the time and place to be restored. But the people of Chiapas still live in poverty. Daily I was challenged to be with them as God had called us to "be with" one another in love.

After my trip to Chiapas in 1991, I knew that I must experience the tribulations of the poor in other places. Through my travel with Pastors on different caravans to Chiapas, Cuba, Nicaragua, El Salvador, Honduras, I have gained much compassion for the people and the difficult situations that the accident of their births has given them.

Besides supporting the IFCO/Pastors-for-Peace mission and goals, members of my congregation and community and I have gone on the Cuban Friendshipment caravan in order to experience firsthand the reality of the country, the effects of the blockade on the Cuban people, to make a difference to our neighbors there by offering "a cup of cold water," and to make a difference in our own lives by looking into the eyes of those we have been taught to call our enemies and seeing the "Christ within."

Because of our government's stance on the blockade, Pastors-for-Peace has chosen to take the steps of challenging the policy of all administrations since Eisenhower, even though the blockade has intensified in more recent years. All U.S. citizens go with the understanding that they will be involved in civil disobedience by their presence on this caravan.

In keeping with much of the U.S. foreign policy, the blockade is having the exact opposite effect that our government intends. The last several administrations have intended to break the spirit of the Cubans, but instead the Cuban people are even more determined, more focused, and more committed to upholding the ideals of their revolution. They see our homeless, our millions without health coverage, and they do not understand it.

We must learn to see ourselves as God's people in spite of arbitrary borders. We are one fragile earth, and we must learn to love one another in dignity and peace. I believe that we in the U.S. are a vital part of the history and the future of our Latin American neighbors. Decisions made here can have profound effects there.

My own life is richer for the experiences with Pastors. I have learned so much:

1. I learned to ride on a musty old school bus. These break down quite frequently and I have rich memories of riding, eating, being creative in ways to sleep. Watching the horrific sights of animals, villages, families being swept away broke our hearts. Learning the corruption of the governments along the way reinforced my skepticism of the structure of governments and reinforced my belief in the hope of humankind. I learned that love, laughter, and tears transcend the barriers we so often build.

2. In my life I had read, studied, taught, preached, and prayed about the faith of a just God. For the first time, I had spent a month living those words in ways I could never have imagined. "Feeding the hungry and giving a cup of cold water to my neighbor" began to take on new and more concrete meaning for me. I believe this is true for all persons who travel on any kind of mission trip. We receive more blessings than we are ever able to give in return.

3. With this fire and conviction in my heart, I have been graced with a ministry of Micah 6:6-8 and the Beatitudes. I have been able to work, listen, and teach with others in congregations, communities, veterans, and hospice about the meaning of "being with" and "solidarity." I learned stories and the power of lives that are willing to take risks and lock horns with power. I have learned, with others in faith, to become that person who is willing to risk, and lock horns with power. I was blessed to be a part of a group that taught me what it means to be a bridge between what we talk about as an ideal way of life and the way we actually live out our lives.

IFCO/Pastors is the ecumenical organization that has graced the lives of so many people in this and other countries. Its roots have grown deep and its fruits have been rich over the past 40 years. Among other community programs, P4P has worked as a hands-on program in New Orleans following the Hurricane, with the people of Nicaragua, Honduras, El Salvador, and protesting the war in Iraq, Kuwait, and the blockade in Cuba. Since that time P4P has continued to be like a thorn in the heart of those who would prevent Pastors from delivering tons of material aid and the message of hope and love to our neighbors who are in need of a cup of cold water.

We communicated the message of Pastors through our church board, and then publicly announced our intentions. We did this by word of mouth and through written publicity. We offered education about the program of Pastors, such as where the caravan would be headed, what aid would be needed, and why Pastors was going to a certain destination. We did not want people to be confused about the issue we had chosen to support.

Our initial task was: 1) to inspire; 2) to educate our people about what the needs of the political and justice issues are and the situation of the country where the caravan would be going so that our members could know the risks and choose their response; and 3) to be involved in supporting Pastors, even if that meant at some point they might be involved in some level of discomfort, or even "civil disobedience." Each year our members can offer to be hosts for the caravan, and everyone can collect supplies and financial goods to be sent along the way.

In addition to involving our own congregation, we wanted to involve other churches. The uniqueness of the methods of the Pastors caravans makes this easier because each year different groups can host *caravanistas* as they come through their area and learn from those who are living that experience. Many from both our own congregation and from others have been inspired to experience service with Pastors first-hand by collecting goods, hosting *caravanistas* in their homes, and even traveling with a caravan.

On the caravans we realized that when dealing with different cultures and people who do not know one another and who are not quite sure of their roles, decisions had to be finally made by one person, our leader. It is not an easy choice to make and caused some difficulty. For example, after Hurricane Mitch people wanted to give supplies along the way. There was dissension. We always attempted to make decisions by consensus. However, when that was not going to happen and we needed to be on our way, the group had to rely on its leader. I have seen this happen time after time under the spiritual and wise leadership of Lucius Walker.

This program is still facing challenges and is still experiencing the breath of the Spirit blowing through our country and our world. As the economy of the world changes, so does the ability and willingness of people and communities to respond to the needs of others. They continue to reach out to young and old, people of all faiths, laity and clergy with a message of the prophets and the beatitudes.

About the Author

Rev Diane Baker is an ordained minister with the Christian Church (Disciples of Christ). She currently works as a hospice chaplain and a minister of outreach in the First Community Church, United Church of Christ/Congregational in Dallas, Texas. She has received the Distinguished Service Award from IFCO/Pastors for Peace and the Peacemaker of the Year Award from the Dallas Peace Center.

Community Organizing For A Just Response to Violence
By Donald Bredthauer

On a December day in 2007, a shooting at a Von Maur department store in a shopping center in suburban Omaha shook the community out of complacency. Eight people were killed and several were injured, some seriously injured. The shooter was an emotionally disturbed young man who, after the killing spree, turned his gun on himself.

People were alarmed and frightened. Gun violence, let alone this kind of extensive violence, ran against the general sense that violence was not common in this part of Omaha. So this tragedy had the community's full attention. The multiple deaths and the serious injuries raised questions. How could this happen? How could it have been prevented? Attention by the media and by the mostly white suburban communities raised additional questions in the minority community in Omaha where there had been a significant increase in violence the preceding few months including 30 shootings in July alone. Where was the outcry then? Why did it take the violence at Von Maur to get everyone's attention?

In response to the anger and frustration that had surfaced around this issue, Omaha Together One Community (OTOC) helped to organize a meeting with several clergy and a few laity at Clair Memorial United Methodist Church. Half of us were white and half were African American. It was a mix of male and female.

It was not a comfortable gathering. There were stories of violence and shootings in Omaha and about the unfair perception that this was primarily a problem for the African American community. There was anger about how the news media often added to that perception. In fact, one television station had announced that the one responsible for the shooting at Von Maur was black before the facts were in. It turned out he was white. Much of the anger that day was directed to the white clergy who were present. Why hadn't we done more to call attention to the violence in Omaha and how it affected the minority community before the Von Maur tragedy? Where had we been? This was the most direct conversation about the continuing racial divide in our city that I've been a part of.

One of the stories told that day pointed to the paralysis of inaction in a vivid way. Thelma Simms, a member of Clair Memorial, spoke of a shooting outside the daycare center where she worked. She said the clergy came the next day and prayed. But nothing else happened. The primary question with which all of us left the meeting was; "Would we do something more than pray about it this time?"

The Von Maur violence led to the exposure of institutional racism and made clear that violence was a painful reality in all parts of our city. OTOC had already scheduled a meeting where the larger community would come together to hear the pain and to pray. The gathering in the basement of Clair Memorial Church changed what would happen at that meeting a week or so later where 160 clergy and laity from 50 congregations all over Omaha came together. Yes, we did pray and we remembered <u>ALL</u> of those who had died during the previous year, mostly through gun violence, by naming them one by one. But we also began a public conversation about how to respond and what to do next. A subsequent meeting was scheduled where individuals told stories about violence throughout the city—rapes, shootings, robberies and homicides and offered their thoughts about solutions. Could we make a difference in reducing the level of violence, especially street violence? Did we have the ability to act? Did we have enough power to bring a workable response to our elected city officials?

Next OTOC, in collaboration with a few non-member congregations, expanded the public conversation by holding a series of four meetings with people in all parts of the city to listen to their experiences of violence. Over 500 people attended. After those gatherings OTOC organized research actions with police, with schools, with leaders in job training programs and with the media to share what we had been hearing, to ask questions and to deepen our understanding about violence in our city. Growing out of that research, groups formed to determine how best to take action. One group focused on jobs, another on after school programs, another on neighborhood revitalization, and another on summer recreation activities for youth.

The OTOC steering committee chose summer recreation activities for youth as a priority for our first step because we believed it held the most realistic chance for making a difference sooner rather than later. There was already a city program called Sun Dawgs, a free summer recreation program with 33 sites open to youths aged 6-15 administered by the city. OTOC had a history of involvement with this program, having run a pilot project that led to its creation several years ago. We felt Sun Dawgs could be expanded to respond more specifically to the issue of violence.

With that focus OTOC organized door-to-door walks with one on one visits in a targeted area around the Holy Name Catholic parish, an OTOC member congregation and the local site for the Sun Dawgs program. Questions were asked. Have you experienced violence? Do you feel safe? What would you like to see happen to improve things for kids? What we heard were stories like the mother who worked two jobs and worried about what would happen to her children, ages 8 and 10, during the summer. We also heard how street violence increased in the summer when kids weren't in school. We heard that people often didn't know their neighbors across the street from them. Several did not know about the Sun Dawgs program. These conversations were critical to building trust and to learning more.

At the Holy Name site for Sun Dawgs there was an attendance increase of 8% over the previous summer. Susan Kuhlmann, a Holy Name parishioner and co-chair of OTOC's response-to-violence committee doesn't believe that was coincidence. She believes it was a direct result of the one on one visits. Mark Darby, Project Organizer with

OTOC, believes organized activities at the Holy Name site planned by OTOC also made a difference. Someone worked with youth coaching basketball. That motivated 15-year- old Jason Dyer who said "I get out of bed and look forward to it every morning." Added to basketball was some teaching on conflict management. As a result we saw teenagers teaching others how to get along. A nurse taught first aid and college students served as mentors.

A key part of our strategy at the Holy Name site was to demonstrate what could happen in the Sun Dawgs program to address youth violence. With the success of that program, key leaders in OTOC scheduled a visit with the mayor and other city officials about expanding the hours at two Sun Dawgs sites the next summer and utilizing a proven anti-violence curriculum with age specific programming and an evaluation component. It was determined that the cost for this pilot project in the summer of 2009 would be $24,000. The mayor decided to include it in the city's budget proposal.

With that, OTOC organized an action with the city council at the budget hearing. Knowing there would be resistance by some council members who had reservations about the program we knew the turn-out from OTOC member congregations would be critical to success. Nearly 100 people crowded into the city council chamber wearing bright yellow stickers that simply read, "Yes to Youth." A city council member expressed surprise about the attendance commenting that the previous year only 12 people showed up. OTOC leaders were prepared to speak to the council in support of the program indicating that youth who participate in organized activities are less likely to be involved in violence. Rev. Michael Williams of Risen Son Baptist Church asked, "What would we rather see in the hands of Omaha youth; basketballs or guns?" Rev. Jason Emerson of All Saints Episcopal Church said the $24,000 was a public safety investment "that shows moral leadership." At a subsequent meeting the city council approved the proposal. OTOC will not run the program. That is the city's job. But you can be sure that OTOC will monitor it closely.

While this victory may seem modest in some ways it was important not just for the positive benefit at two Sun Dawgs sites but because it lays the groundwork for more substantial victories. OTOC is already planning for the future with the goal of increased funding to expand the program to ten sites. Additionally OTOC groups are working on how to form safer neighborhoods, economic alternatives to selling drugs and establishing family wellness programs.

Studies have shown that organized ways for neighbors to have one on one interaction with each other and to share a sense of power to solve problems will have a positive effect on the level of violence and a sense of pride in their neighborhood. Researchers have shown that neighborhoods with improved quality and depth of relationships ("collective efficacy") were 30% less likely to have experienced violent crime and 40% less likely to have experienced homicide.[1] Many scholars believe that grass-root organizations using relational power are key factors.

Community organizing is about "collective efficacy" or simply "community" in the best sense of what community means. Community organizing teaches the art of building and using relational power for justice and the common good. So how does it happen? The above story about the "first step" response of OTOC to violence in Omaha provides a snapshot example of community organizing at work but perhaps more information would be helpful to the reader using OTOC as a model.

OTOC is a broad-based, multiethnic and interfaith organization. Members are institutions, mostly of congregations: Roman Catholic, Protestant, Unitarian and Jewish at this point. It began in the early 1990s. The congregation I was serving at the time, First United Methodist, was among the first to commit money and leaders to build this organization. The persistent themes throughout the Hebrew and Christian scriptures to love God and neighbor and to do God's justice provide the underlying faith foundation for this work. We often recall a verse found in Jeremiah; "But seek the welfare of the city where I have sent you into exile, and pray to the Lord on its behalf, for in its welfare you will find your welfare." (Jeremiah 29:7)

In our fragmented society OTOC brings people together across the lines that tend to divide us: race, economics, religion and geography. Together we learn about issues that we and our neighbors throughout the city are concerned about. We do this through individual conversations (one on one visits), research committees and regular house meeting campaigns which often involve hundreds of gatherings of eight to ten people each. Through the disciplined practice of these skills, people build relationships of trust.

Once an issue has been identified, strategies and actions are planned by members of the OTOC steering committee. We have held elected officials accountable through tough but always respectful public discourse. We have stood with others at a meat packing plant to support union elections for workers. We have organized turnouts at city council meetings to support a living wage ordinance, increased funding for libraries, and increased awareness and funding of sewer separation projects in older neighborhoods. We have worked with officials on something as simple as expanding the waiting area at the local Immigration Office. OTOC, by acting collaboratively with other allies, teaches us as citizens how to stand up for ourselves and our self interest through the exercise of relational power rather than expecting someone else to take care of us. In the process we create positive change through collective action for the common good.[2]

While clergy credential the organization by making clear the connection between our faith tradition and the work of OTOC and sometimes by putting a public face on OTOC through the clergy caucus, laity primarily lead the organization. Each member congregation is expected to have a Leadership Team that will regularly meet with leaders from other OTOC congregations and keep the congregation informed about the issues and about larger meetings where congregational members can learn about what's happening and how they can support the action to address a particular issue.

The organization is supported primarily through dues from member congregations to pay the salaries of a lead organizer and a modest staff as well as office expenses. The primary job of the lead organizer is to teach us the skills required for this work, not to do our work for us. The dues also support a contract with the Industrial Areas Foundation[3] which prepares the lead organizer for this work and provides training for organizational leaders. Beyond providing funds for these purposes, dues are important to assure ownership. No public funds are used to support the organization.

Small victories, such as the one described above regarding violence in Omaha, are often critical as an organizing strategy because they build confidence and develop new leaders. For example, Rev. Michael

Williams who spoke to the city council and who had never engaged in this kind of activity before now feels that organizing in this way is "the best way to get things done." A modest victory can also help build the organization. Because of new relationships formed around the above action, one more congregation became an OTOC member and two more are in the process of deciding on membership. New leaders from these congregations will be identified and trained to listen and will learn how to continue this important work.

My 15 plus years of experience with OTOC, have demonstrated many times that this is "the best way to get things done," things that really matter in the life of our community. However, often overlooked is how OTOC strengthens the life of the local congregation itself. The leadership development for organizing that occurs through training and experience is the key to that happening. As clergy and laity together learn how to respect and work with others who are different from them, how to organize, how to run house meetings, how to do research, how to ask the right questions and how to keep focused on what's most important, you can be certain those skills will translate back to your own congregation. And those leaders teach others how to lead by their example.

But it is not just about getting things done. As we pray and work together, as we create the space for conversation, as we build relationships we are transformed to use our power to be the people God calls us to be: a people who do justice and walk humbly with God. I believe community organizing is one of the most effective ways for a congregation, working with other congregations, to participate in God's justice work at the local level.

Notes

[1] Eyal Press, *Can Block Clubs Block Despair?* American Prospect, May 16, 2007.

[2] Some information in this article about OTOC was taken from a brochure about the organization entitled *Democracy is not a Spectator Sport.*

[3] The Industrial Areas Foundation works with similar projects across the United States including Texas, New Mexico, Arizona, California, Oklahoma, Louisiana, Iowa, Illinois, and New York.

About the Author

Donald Bredthauer is a United Methodist pastor. He is affiliated with First United Methodist Church in Omaha, Nebraska from which he retired as pastor in 2000. He was one of the original co-chairs of Omaha Together One Community and continues to be active in the organization.

Doing Justice: Issues and Strategies
By Lauren Ekdahl

There have been many opportunities for prophetic witness on justice issues in my ministry since graduating from Saint Paul School of Theology in 1974. My appointment to Dakota City/ Homer Charge in Northeast Nebraska gave immediate urgency to this part of my theological training as a witness to the gospel. A labor dispute between Iowa Beef Processors, a two billion dollar boxed beef processing company, escalated into a strike in February1977 approximately two and one half months after I entered this, my first full time appointment. The strike would continue for some fourteen months. It put nearly two thousand workers on picket lines with no prospect of "good faith" negotiation on the horizon despite several months of wrangling between the company and Amalgamated Meat Cutters Union 222. The suffering among communities of the Siouxland Metropolitan Area of northeast Nebraska, western Iowa and southeast South Dakota was becoming critical. The prospect of violence on the picket line or in acts of frustration in the communities was building daily. My appointment to Dakota City/ Homer Charge made me the only resident pastor in the home office community of Iowa Beef Processors Inc. I was confronted daily by the tensions of family life where loss of income was being experienced, and community services were being strained to the breaking point. Nearly one hundred State Patrol Officers were stationed at the entrance to the IBP Plant each morning to maintain order and forestall the violence that had beset prior disputes. I prayed and agonized over the situation for some time before I finally decided to act.

I was active in a community organizing effort known as the Siouxland Metropolitan Ministries alongside other socially conscious religious leaders in the area. I took the concern I carried about the strike to this group. I presented the argument that if we truly represented a justice ministry we needed to act to mobilize clergy and laity to call for justice by calling IBP and Amalgamated Meat Cutters 222 to good faith bargaining in this devastating strike. I managed to convince a small core group to join me in developing an invitation to clergy to act. The result was the development of <u>Siouxland Religious Committee for Community and Justice</u>. Our first task was the development and distribution of a letter to leaders, clergy and laity, to join the effort by attending an organizational meeting at the Dakota City United Methodist Church. We proposed as a beginning strategy the following: That we, as persons who are part of the Siouxland Church Community, attempt to awaken greater concern in the wider community for this situation by the following means.

First, releasing a statement: "The Church in general, in its variety of denominational organization, has always seen itself as "called" to care for the welfare of persons and their families. Indeed, the church is a prime promoter of healthy family life, along with many other elements of our community. We believe it is thus both valid and crucial that we as members of the church community in Siouxland strongly express our concern for a situation which is having a detrimental impact on family life, but about which there has been little public discussion or expression of concern."

We then went on in the statement to state the various concerns we had for family life, strains on social service agencies in the area, and concern over community commerce and social wellbeing. The statement continued: "We believe that the relationship of Iowa Beef Processors to its union employees exists not on an island, but in the midst of this community's life. It affects this entire community, directly or indirectly, in the impact on family life as well as the economics of this area." We concluded our statement with: "We call on Iowa Beef Processors, which we perceive to have a more powerful position in this situation, to resume bargaining in good faith in order that the strike might be concluded."

The second part of the organizational effort centered on a statement to be presented to each congregation and parish in Siouxland and a request that persons (church members) be asked to register their expressions of concern by signing the statement.

The third component consisted of gathering a large group of church persons to publicly discuss our concerns that could be publicly conveyed to both the Company and the Union.

This initial effort at organizing resulted, as indicated, in the establishment of the Siouxland Religious Committee for Community and Justice. What followed was a series of statements released to the news media through press conferences held in the fellowship hall of the Dakota City United Methodist Church. All statements called on IBP and the Union to end the deadlock and enter into good faith negotiations. Local newspapers such as the weekly South Sioux City Star and the daily Sioux City Journal found it difficult to embrace the concern expressed by clergy as anything other than meddling in something we could not possibly understand. To their credit, however, they did respond to our called press conferences and did report our concerns through their news outlets. Their editorials, on the other hand, repeatedly questioned our right to be involved and in some instances focused on questioning the integrity of spokespersons reporting Committee statements. As chief spokesperson for the Committee I often found my motives questioned as well as the leadership I was giving my church. The following is an example of a response I made to such an attack:

"Dear Editor:

The question published in the Action Editor Section of the April 13th edition of the South Sioux City Star relating to the Dakota City church I serve and my personal concern over the I.B.P. strike is an incredible 'Cheap-Shot'. I am amazed that the Action Editor failed to document the basic premise that prompted it. I cannot recall a time when Union members have been pictured around the Dakota City United Methodist Church.

Public statements made with regard to the labor dispute at I.B.P. have consistently called both parties to a "peaceful" resolution of their differences by use of the negotiating options offered them in an honorable collective bargaining posture. In short, we called both parties to be "ethical" in their negotiating style and to exhibit some professionalism in their relationship toward each other and the community.

I have not asked the Dakota City United Methodist Church to endorse the concerns expressed by the Siouxland Religious Committee for Community and Justice. Rather, I have sought the guidance of the United Methodist *Book of Discipline* which contains a section called "Social Principles" which reads in Para. 73, statement B, page 96: "COLLECTIVE BARGAINING --- We support the right of public and private (including farm, government, institutional, and domestic) employees and employers to organize for collective bargaining into unions and other groups of their own choosing. Further, we support the right of both parties to protection in so doing, and their responsibility to bargain in good faith within the framework of the public interest. In order that the rights of all members of the society may be maintained and promoted, we support innovative bargaining procedures that include representatives of the public interest in negotiation and settlement of labor-management contracts including some that may lead to forms of judicial resolution of issues.

Finally, I would state that what I have said, I have said publicly over my own signature. If religious leadership means anything to persons of religious convictions, it is based upon a pastor's willingness to bring theological insight and understanding to bear upon the problems which destroy personal esteem and right relations with God and our neighbors. The ministry entrusted to me is not a call to preach "only what people want to hear." It is a call to proclaim "what people need to hear" in order to live a lifestyle consistent with the faith they espouse. I have a poster hanging in my office that reads: 'If you are not a part of the solution, you are a part of the problem.' Ethical behavior is a valid concern in business and society generally.

Grace and Peace, Rev. Lauren D. Ekdahl"

As the strike continued we decided to appeal to the National Labor Relations Board to intervene with "Binding Arbitration." We suggested that the Union make such an appeal and the Union followed that suggestion. Iowa Beef Processors argued against such an action. Once again we called a press conference and stated our position with a statement released on March 8,1978, signed by the fifteen members of the Committee:

"Once again we call upon Iowa Beef Processors Inc. of Dakota City to open the way for a peaceful settlement of their present labor dispute by making use of the peaceful processes of Collective Bargaining. Iowa Beef's present position is an invitation to expressions of violence precisely at the point where they have shut the door to any reasonable method for seeking agreement. Instead of addressing the problems with an eye toward community and justice, they chose to develop an atmosphere of violent confrontation and then exploit it to their own public relations advantage.

We would publicly condemn as unconscionable any acts of violence by either party to this dispute. Such actions are counterproductive to any peaceful resolution of the problem. We would remind persons in this community, however, that closing the options for peaceful settlement is an act of violence in itself. We would remind the media that sensationalizing one aspect of violence while overlooking the other more subtle expressions of violence is in itself an act of violence perpetrated upon this community.

Once again we ask for a <u>credible</u> explanation from Iowa Beef Processors of the reasons 'Binding Arbitration' is not deemed feasible at this time. We are completely unwilling to accept their statement without proper explanation beyond their pronouncements of self-interest. We doubt that there are any <u>credible</u> reasons when measured against 'ethical decisions' bearing the weight of a reasoned response to 'Justice in the Community' as a necessary element of interest and concern."

The strike was finally settled on July 27, 1978, with the workers returning on August 3. The Sioux City Journal reported that the Union felt the final agreement met most of their goals. The Siouxland Religious Committee for Community and Justice had done its best to educate citizens and elevate relationships in the community above rhetoric that would incite violence. It was our intent to push the Company and the Union toward a deeper awareness of their role in community life and to be responsive to community needs in a caring and ethical way. The Committee disbanded with a celebration of our common bond and a successful outcome. We did not solicit approbation for the Committee nor did we receive any from the public media or those most directly involved in the conflict. It was enough to know that at long last it was over.

I received the approbation of my District Superintendent, Rev. Hughes B. Morris, who stood staunchly with me through the entire process as did Nebraska Bishop Monk Bryan. I was nominated for and received the first Iowa Chapter of the Methodist Federation for Social Action "Social Justice Award." The letter read that the award is presented " …to someone who has made a significant social witness in the area of social justice concerns." I received the award at the MFSA banquet held at the time of the Iowa Annual Conference in 1978. The award is one of many cherished reminders of my call to ministry as a person who must challenge persons to a life congruent with the gospel we proclaim.

I was told by many church folk that I would ruin the Dakota City and Homer United Methodist churches by involving myself in this dispute. I am happy to report that our churches grew during that time and my personal credibility as a pastor was enhanced. I did receive letters from some clergy in the area who questioned my call and my understanding of ministry. One such correspondence was sent to Bishop Monk Bryan questioning him as to his awareness over what I was "up to." The District Superintendent brought his response to my churches to be read to them by my D.S. before the Bishop mailed the response to the Senior Pastor of a large church in Sioux City, Iowa. The essence of the letter read was: "Yes, I know what Rev. Ekdahl is doing. Yes, I approve of what Rev. Ekdahl is doing. No, I do not have any plans to move Rev. Ekdahl anytime soon. Grace and Peace, Bishop Monk Bryan." The church members gave great applause to that letter after it was read in our service, which greatly warmed my heart and gave me encouragement.

About the Author

Rev. Lauren D. Ekdahl is a pastor in the Nebraska Conference of the United Methodist Church. He served forty years as a social activist pastor seeking to connect the United Methodist Social Principles with active engagement in the communities where he served. He was twice appointed as a District Superintendent before retirement in 2007. He continues to address social issues of importance in Nebraska and the nation.

What Is a Church – If It Is Not a Sanctuary?
By John Fife

Since its founding in 1906, Southside Presbyterian Church in Tucson, Arizona has always been on the margin. Southside was organized as a mission church for Native Americans when they were excluded from living with "civilized" folks in the city and from worshiping in the Presbyterian Church.

Following World War II, the city had grown around the church, the barrio was the oldest and poorest in Tucson, and the congregation included Mexican-Americans. In 1956 an African American pastor was called. Southside Church became a multicultural worshipping community known for its support of civil rights organizing, desegregation of public facilities, and the integration of public schools. That faithful history was critically important as it undertook the task of congregational renewal.

When I was called to serve as pastor in 1969, Southside had become marginalized again through neglect and attrition. The congregation had not had a pastor for several years, and the few remaining members were struggling to keep it open. The challenge before us was apparent: rebuild a viable, multi-cultural worshiping congregation and begin once again to serve the needs of the barrio. The worship became spirit-filled and joyful as a gifted African-American gospel musician agreed to become the music director.

Southside hosted a Head Start school for neighborhood children, helped to organize the community to build a neighborhood Recreation Center, and formed a non-profit low-income housing corporation for Native American families – the first in the nation. An early test occurred when the congregation's lay leader and I were arrested for trespassing when we delivered a long list of treaty violations by the government to the U.S. Attorney.

By 1980 Southside Church had renewed the congregation. A vital, multi-cultural worship experience and youth program now filled the buildings, trusted relationships had been rebuilt with the community and community organizations, and we were gaining an identity as a community of faith willing to take risks for social justice and peacemaking. It's a good thing that we had those ten years for renewal, because a storm was thundering south of the border that would test our faith and commitment to the gospel.

That storm took the form of death squads, torture and disappearance; and the assassination of an Archbishop, priests, nuns, and thousands of catechists in El Salvador. In Guatemala the military massacred hundreds of villages of Mayan people in the highlands, the most horrendous slaughter of indigenous peoples since the Spanish conquest. Refugees fleeing this repression and terror in Central America swelled from a trickle to a flood in the early 1980's. Crossing the U.S.-Mexico border without documents, they were being captured by Border Patrol and Immigration Agents, locked up in jails and detention centers, and deported in handcuffs to the tender mercies of the military and death squads of El Salvador and Guatemala.

Southside Presbyterian Church began to respond to this crisis in human rights by helping to organize a task force under the Tucson Ecumenical Council to provide legal aid services to the refugees. A weekly prayer service in solidarity with the persecuted church in Central America was initiated. Within a year, a devastating truth became apparent: the United States Government refused to recognize these people who were fleeing the massacres and wars as refugees. The reason for this was equally devastating: the U.S. was in political, economic, and military support of the death squads.

A Quaker, Jim Corbett, put the ethical question clearly before the pastor and congregation of Southside. He pointed to two historic moments. The first was the faithfulness of the Abolition Movement to help runaway slaves through the Underground Railroad. The tragic failure of the church in Europe to protest Jewish refugees was the second. "We cannot allow that to happen on our border in our time," Corbett stated. He continued, "Because the U.S. government takes the position that aiding undocumented Salvadoran and Guatemalan refugees in this country is a felony, we have no middle ground between collaboration and resistance. When the government itself sponsors the crucifixion of entire peoples, and then makes it a felony to shelter those seeking refuge, law abiding protest merely trains us to live with atrocity."

The Southside Church Session responded by opening the church as a shelter for refugees, and some members joined Corbett and their pastor in smuggling refugees safely across the border. It took the Border Patrol about six months to learn about our efforts, and they sent us a clear ultimatum, "Stop or we will indict you." The only ethical response under the circumstances was to go public and hope for support from the community of faith when we were indicted. After a three month process of prayer, theological and Biblical reflection, and legal consultation, the congregation voted by secret ballot to become a Sanctuary for refugees from Central America.

On March 24, 1982, a family from El Salvador was received into the Sanctuary of the church. A letter to the Attorney General of the U.S. explained, "We take this action because we believe the current policy and practice of the U.S. government with regard to Central American refugees is illegal and immoral. We believe that justice and mercy require that people of conscience exercise our God-given right to aid anyone fleeing from persecution and murder. Obedience to God requires this of us all."

The motivation for Southside Church's declaration of Sanctuary was multi-faceted.

BIBLICAL: The scriptures were clear and compelling. From the Torah covenant to Matthew 25, the alien/stranger was to be protected.

THEOLOGICAL: Justice and mercy required this witness. Sanctuary was an historic tradition of the church.

ETHICAL: Sanctuary became a witness of active, non-violent resistance to governmental violations of human rights.

LEGAL: The Reagan administration was in violation of U.S. Refugee Law.

Much to our astonishment we were not indicted, but a movement had begun. Churches and synagogues, compelled by their faith and ethical responsibility, began to declare Sanctuary for refugees. An underground railroad, in the tradition of the Abolition Movement, developed the capacity to move refugees from the borderlands across the U.S. and on to Canada. Seventeen cities, including New York, Chicago, and Los Angeles, declared themselves "cities of sanctuary" and instructed their public officials not to cooperate with Federal Immigration Agents. Stanford University became the first of a series of educational institutions to become a Sanctuary. Within two years, 237 churches and synagogues were leading the movement, and Bishops and denominations had declared their support. The idea of church as Sanctuary spread to Europe as churches in Germany, France, England, the Netherlands, and Switzerland protected refugees threatened with deportation. A movement had been born!

Two other radical changes occurred as a result. One was spiritual and theological. The refugees brought with them a new way of reading and understanding the Bible – through the eyes of the poor and the suffering. The churches provided a safe and public place where refugees could tell their stories to the community. But the refugees taught North American Christians how to read the Bible from the experience of the poor and the persecuted – not the experience of the privileged. For the pastor and the members of Southside Presbyterian Church, it was a conversion experience. We understood for the first time that Jesus was present in the poor and in the refugee at our door and that as we did to the least of these, we did to the crucified and risen Christ. Sanctuary was no longer an ethical or theological concept; it was a spiritual act of faith in the presence of Jesus.

The second change was in the role of the church when government violates human rights. After World War II, the Nuremberg Trials of Nazi officials had established a new legal principle. That principle overturned the defense that "just following orders" of the nation-state was an individual's ultimate legal responsibility. Nuremberg established the responsibility of all people to maintain human rights and international law when nation-states were the violators. What Nuremberg failed to establish was the social base to implement that principle. The Sanctuary Movement, for the first time, recognized faith communities as that social and institutional base for implementation.

In 1984 as the Sanctuary Movement grew in numbers and influence, the government decided to move to a strategy of arrests and indictments. Two volunteers in Texas were charged with transporting illegal aliens. Southside Presbyterian Church, along with at least five other churches in Arizona and Sonora, Mexico, were infiltrated with undercover agents and paid informants. Tape recordings were secretly made of worship services, Bible-study groups, and meetings in the churches. In 1985 the tapes were utilized to indict sixteen volunteers in Arizona: two priests, four nuns, the pastor of Southside, and several lay people. During the seven-month trial, the number of churches and synagogues declaring Sanctuary more than doubled to over 580, and legislation to stop deportations to El Salvador and Guatemala gained momentum in Congress.

The defendants were convicted in court only because the judge excluded from the courtroom any mention of U.S. Refugee Law and the conditions in Central America. Taking the initiative, the Sanctuary Movement filed a civil suit in Federal Court against the Attorney General of the U.S. for his violations of refugee law. Just before that civil suit was tried, an agreement was reached with the Justice Department: all deportations to El Salvador and Guatemala were ended; all undocumented refugees from El Salvador and Guatemala were given work permits; and a series of reforms of the political asylum process were implemented. The Sanctuary Movement had succeeded in protecting tens of thousands of vulnerable refugees and in changing U.S. immigration and refugee policy.

Today, Southside Presbyterian Church continues to minister from the margin. Still located in the oldest and poorest barrio in Tucson, the diversity of the congregation has expanded beyond multi-cultural. Gay and lesbian members are ordained Elders, and the homeless serve as Deacons alongside physicians and teachers. A worship center utilizing Native American architecture has been built, and a new education building serves both the Head Start program and the church school. Twice a week a program for the homeless and migrants provides showers, clean clothes, and a meal for 100 – 150 persons. For seven years Southside has based an organization called Samaritans at the church. Volunteer doctors, nurses, and Spanish-speakers go out each day in 4-wheel-drive vehicles with food, water, and emergency medical gear to provide life-saving humanitarian aid to migrant workers crossing the Sonoran Desert. A medical clinic and shelter for sick and injured migrants is located next to the pastor's office. Every morning undocumented day laborers gather in the church parking lot to seek work. They have organized themselves to end wage and workplace exploitation, and the church provides a sanctuary from Border Patrol or police raids.

From the margin, Southside Church continues to form community with the poor and marginalized in their struggle for justice and liberation.

Jesus is surely present in the Holy Communion that is celebrated there. What is a church if it is not such a sanctuary?

About the Author

John M. Fife served as pastor of Southside Presbyterian Church in Tucson, Arizona until his retirement in 2005. He was elected Moderator of the General Assembly of the Presbyterian Church (U.S.A.) in 1992. He currently volunteers with "No More Deaths," a humanitarian aid organization saving lives of undocumented migrant workers in the Sonoran Desert region of the borderlands.

Everyday is Earth Day at Northaven UMC: Becoming Stewards of God's Creation
By Eric Folkerth and Jan Sanders

The creation stories of our tradition frame us as "stewards" of God's good creation. In a real sense, then, "Christian stewardship" means far more than what we do with our financial resources and even more than what we do with our time. Ultimately, a key measure of our "stewardship" is how we care for and love God's good earth.

The connection between our life of faith and care for the environment has a spiritual core. The beauty of God's creation is one of the ways many people experience the direct presence of God. So, care for the world is not simply a duty forced upon us as an obligation but a direct way to foster our connection with God.

Many of Jesus' parables and stories had direct connection to the natural world. He told stories about seeds, fields, birds, rocks and mountains. Undoubtedly, a part of this was because these would have been familiar symbols to his listeners.

But when Jesus tells us to "consider the lilies of the field. ... consider the ravens of the air," it is not simply because doing this helps reduce our worry, but also because such meditation and prayer connect us with how God is visible in the natural world and that God's gifts are plentiful, beautiful and miraculous. Jesus himself prepared for his ministry by going into the wilderness. Might we benefit from such a retreat to connect with God? What a powerful Biblical reminder that we should protect our wild places.

Northaven United Methodist Church members have a long, rich history of connecting care for the environment with their faith. Our story starts with simple steps taken years ago that have grown into expanding circles of action. Some of the early actions consisted of challenging local governments to change. In more recent years, our activities have been centered on what we, as individuals and families, can do to make an environmental impact as a witness to our faith.

More than 20 years ago, long before the city of Dallas implemented a comprehensive recycling program, Northaven Church began recycling on its own. We collected recycled newspapers from the congregation and the neighborhood in a big trailer on our parking lot. Volunteers staffed the trailer, even in the scorching summer months which was a labor of love. Slowly the Dallas City Council came around, encouraged by a coalition formed to advocate for more environmental action. A Northaven member who had served on the Mayor's Task Force on Recycling took a leadership role in that effort. Northaven's pastor and lay leadership supported the effort.

Advocacy at the city level came only after careful analysis and study. Attention was paid to the impact of the city's policies in a number of areas: cost efficiency, impact on the poor, noise and safety, job security for the city's sanitation workers, impact on air quality, public accountability, and the openness of the contract process. The process ended with a single stream collection of recyclables to be hauled by city sanitation workers using city equipment, resulting in cost efficiency, flexibility and accountability. Significant materials are now diverted from the landfill. Air quality is taken into account when fleet cars and trucks are acquired and the routes and number of pickups are planned. As time passed, the elected city leaders and staff became more mindful of good environmental practices in many other policy areas, such as the acquisition of cars for police and fire departments. In more recent years, the city has mandated specific green requirements for new construction within the city and for new regulations about energy and water conservation.

In those early years Northaven involved our youth in educating on recycling and environmental action. The youth collected metal, glass and plastic and made trips to a suburban collection center. Youth teams loved smashing the glass and stomping aluminum cans while learning to answer the question, "Why is this important?" Another 1980's educational effort utilized our youth and adult members to do testing for acid rain in north Texas. Led by an experienced scientist and church member, our youth did simple chemical analysis and discovered that acid rain was present in this area and was a real problem. It was shown to damage plant life and the paint on automobiles..

This legacy of environmental action has grown and spread throughout our congregation in recent years. We annually celebrate "Earth Day" on the Sunday closest to April 22. Litanies, sermons, and hymns are always chosen to build the theological core for environmentalism. The congregation is challenged to take personal and corporate action to restore and protect the environment. In 2006, the church hosted an art installation that was created entirely from "trash" and featured the non-recyclable, stay-in-the-earth-forever, manmade styrofoam. One sculpture piece depicted the Dallas skyline in a flood produced of styrofoam. Dozens of Dallas artists contributed pieces of this "trash art" for the display.

One of the most popular features of these recent "Earth Day Sundays" has been the "Northaven Car Show." Owners of hybrid, and other high MPG vehicles, are invited to bring their cars, "pop the hoods" and collectively display them so the congregation can learn more as they leave the church and head for the parking lot. The clear message is to gently advocate the use of such vehicles as a way to express our faith through what we drive. The first year, the "Car Show" had only four cars. But it has grown each year since, and last year we had over twenty-five cars. Clearly our members are making environmental choices with respect to the cars they drive. Our youth sponsored an "Earth Day Market" that same weekend that raised money for youth programs and was a community outreach that made real the "reuse" part of the recycling mantra, "Reduce, Reuse, Recycle." The garage sale style event successfully diverted items away from the landfill, helped low income families, and raised money for the youth's mission trip. A win-win all the way around! The youth also passed out information about recycling to all who attended.

The 2009 Earth Day at the Northaven celebration featured food we eat and the water we drink. The Church in Society Commission educated the congregation with a Mission Minute delivered during the Sunday worship service on water conservation and the environmental reason for the abolition of plastic bottled water. A "Vegetarian Cook Off Contest" supplanted the usual covered dish church fare, along with an explanation of how eating locally and organically grown foods would favorably impact the environment and our health. To emphasize the theological symbolism of water, the meal blessing included an invitation for the participants to pour water from pitchers on the table and serve one another.

Cleaning our air is made more urgent by global climate change. Northaven has taken steps here as well. Under the leadership of Texas Impact's "Breath of Life" campaign, an "energy audit" of our new building was done. This has resulted not only in reducing the energy we use, but also in reducing our energy costs. For the past two years, Northaven Church has purchased 100 percent "green energy" from its energy provider. The church is a part of an energy contract with the North Texas Conference of the United Methodist Church that allows for at least ten percent "green" energy" for all United Methodist Churches in North Texas. This is believed to be the first time in history that a denominational judicatory has successfully lobbied for the inclusion of such a requirement in an electrical power contract. Churches can pay an extra premium to receive 100 percent "green" power. That premium is approximately 3 percent of our annual electric bill. Northaven's Board of Trustees unanimously endorsed paying the additional premium, despite the cost, and called the decision "a no-brainer" for the congregation. We believe this is simply a sign of how firmly established the desire for environmental action has become in the congregation.

Our working with the statewide membership of Texas Impact is an excellent example of how Northaven has led by example and has been successful in tackling big issues in coalition with others. A current example is the effort to support the development of sustainable energy sources through the support of public policy at the state and national level. Sometimes public policy advocacy means blocking a damaging program. A recent success was advocacy and action in thwarting an effort to bring into being a half dozen new coal powered plants in Texas.

Our church's commitment to environmental stewardship has been public and private, corporate and individual. It has involved changing what we do as individuals, as a church, and as citizens of our city. Throughout this journey we have been pleased at the response of our members, and encourage all churches to consider how powerfully the connection of environmentalism and faith can be for a congregation. It's a clear way to live out our calling to be stewards of God's creation.

About the Authors

Eric Folkerth is a graduate of Perkins School of Theology and has served as pastor of Northaven United Methodist Church in Dallas since 2001. He has been on mission trips over the years to many countries.

Jan Sanders considers her work for peace, justice, and the restoration and protection of the environment as her faith work. She is an active member of the Church in Society Commission of Northaven United Methodist Church.

Who is My Neighbor?
Fulfilling the Great Commandment through Peacemaking
By Barry E. Hughes

I had been appointed to the Asbury United Methodist Church in Bossier City, Louisiana in June 2001. Bossier City is a military community in the fullest sense of the word. The economy is anchored in the existence of Barksdale Air Force Base, the Base to which the President was flown on the day referred to simply as 9-11. But even more important than the economic impact is the influence of Barksdale on the character of this southern town of around 60,000 people. Patriotism, political and theological conservatism, law and order, a high value placed on duty and honor – these attributes are the heart and soul of the community.

It is easy to understand the impact of 9-11 on Bossier City. As pastor of the 1100 member congregation, I had the experience of preaching to parishioners on the Sunday preceding 9-11 who were absent in the weeks and months following due to their deployment to Afghanistan as the "war on terror" began. Emotion-laden language such as beginning a "war with Islam" took firm root in the psyche of the community. Residents may not have known an individual who died in the Twin Towers or the Pentagon or the Pennsylvania countryside, but they did know individuals who were separated from home and friends because of the response of the United States.

As a pastor, especially a pastor new to the congregation, how does one speak of peace in such a time and in such a place? How does one address the misconception of the conflict as a war between the Christian and the Muslim religions? Ultimately the question came to be "What can possibly be done by a group of religious people in a small southern town that would make a stand for peace?"

Realizing that fear and hate are often related to misinformation or ignorance, the hypothesis that would guide this ministry of peace and justice was simple: Knowledge + Experience = Tolerance/Acceptance. If members of the Asbury congregation had the opportunity to learn basic information concerning the religion of Islam, and then had the opportunity to actually meet and interact with local persons who defined their lives by that religion, might attitudes toward Islam as a religion and Muslims as a group be changed? Might such a community action work for peace in the midst of war?

An invitation was issued to the congregation regarding an opportunity to learn about the religion of Islam and to experience interreligious dialogue with Muslim neighbors. (Interestingly enough, it became clear through informal conversations around the church that no parishioners believed that Muslims lived in the greater Shreveport/ Bossier City area. This was particularly surprising in light of the fact that there were two Islamic places of worship in the area!)

Surprisingly, 38 adults responded to the invitation and committed to a process that spread over several months. The participants agreed to a personal interview for the purposes of ascertaining their experience with those persons of another religious tradition. They worshiped together with Jews, Christians, and Muslims at an interfaith worship service sponsored by the local community organizing affiliate of the Industrial Areas Foundation. Each person completed an instrument that measured both attitudes and knowledge related to the religion of Islam.

Five hours of basic instruction in the tenets and history of Islam were shared in a classroom setting. It was stressed at the beginning of each class session that these classes, led by the pastor, would not be the same experience as learning from Muslims who shared the story and faith that defined their lives. This instruction was provided for the elementary purpose of providing participants enough knowledge to ask respectful questions when the dialogue sessions took place.

On two separate evenings the leader of each Muslim group in our community was asked to bring a group of 38 persons, male and female, from their respective faith community to the Asbury Church for a night of dialogue. The program would begin with a presentation by a leader in the Muslim group on the topic, "What we want Christians to know about Islam." Following the presentation, Christians and Muslims would pair up for a time of personal, unscripted conversations around refreshments. When this time came to a close, the groups reassembled for a period of questions and answers around the presentation and conversations.

Following the classes and two experiences of dialogue, participants from all three groups gathered at the local food bank to share in a joint community service action. Then the participants from the Asbury congregation again completed the instrument that measured both attitudes and knowledge related to the religion of Islam.

I was unprepared for the "across the board" changes revealed by the before and after comparison of each participant's instrument. The hypothesis was proven true. The basic knowledge of Islam gained through the classes enabled those persons to experience dialogue with their Muslim neighbors in a non-threatening way. Participants could see where and how misinformation and emotion-laden language had formed their attitudes concerning an entire group of religious persons who lived in their neighborhoods and whose children attended the same schools as their own children. Fear was reduced and new possibilities for thinking about the relationship between Muslims and Christians came to light.

If I were to change this process in any way I would follow each visit from the two Muslim groups with the experience of the Asbury group visiting each Muslim place of worship. (This opportunity was not offered at the time and I chose not to press the issue.) Upon further reflection,

I think that receiving the hospitality of our Muslim neighbors would have been a very special experience for us all. Offering hospitality is one thing; receiving hospitality is a different thing all together. Power is in a different place when these roles are reversed in the relationship.

It seems clear that the major achievement of this action was the real interaction between Christians and Muslims. It was a powerful experience to listen as our Muslim neighbors shared the pain caused by hearing and reading the name of their religion always followed by words such as "extremist" and "terrorist." It was also powerful to experience the graciousness, openness and eagerness of our neighbors to know and understand us better as Christians. There is no substitute for meeting and conversing with a person as "person," as opposed to thinking of them as one of a group.

Theologically, parishioners had to wrestle with several concepts in new ways. First, the idea of peacemaking as an attribute of the Christian life was named. This was not popular in either the political or theological climate of the culture. But if, as William Sloane Coffin declared, peace is in fact "God's most cherished hope for humanity," peacemaking must be upheld as part and parcel of a Christian life. The work of peace must become a part of congregational life if we are to raise up leaders who embrace peace as the desire of their hearts.

Second, the idea of evangelism had to be reexamined. In too many churches, especially those in areas so influenced by revivalism, evangelism is understood only to mean the increasing of the membership roll of a particular congregation. But if evangelism is understood to be the proclamation of the good news of the Kingdom of God, many nuanced facets appear. The many areas of social justice become, instead of an appendage to our work in evangelism, the medium of our proclamation. Peace, justice, workers rights, civil rights, poverty – ministry in all these areas proclaim life as it should be for all God's children. That is evangelism at its best, proclaiming the Kingdom with no motive other than the good of all.

Lastly, the overall understanding of what it means to define one's self as "Christian" had to be addressed. Is it enough to claim the name "Christian," or must one also follow in the way of Christ in one's relationship to others? Can bigotry and hate be reconciled with a person's claim to be a Christian? Do not Christians have a responsibility to work for peace and justice for those who are vulnerable or in peril? What good is our faith if it serves us and us alone? Perhaps this type of dialogue is one real way to fulfill what Jesus called the Great Commandment, to love God with all we are and to love our neighbor as we love ourselves.

These larger theological wrestlings were an important part of this peacemaking experience. Changes in pastoral appointments have ended interfaith work in this congregation at this time, but I am convinced that participants from all three groups will never be quite the same. They were all a part of something important. In their small corner of the world and in their own small way, they took a stand for peace.

About the Author

Rev. Dr. Barry E. Hughes is an Elder in the Louisiana Annual Conference of the United Methodist Church, where he has served an inner city congregation, a church start, and a suburban congregation in a military town where this interreligious experience took place. He is now on the faculty of Perkins School of Theology at Southern Methodist University.

Combatting Sweatshops: How Congregations Can Participate in a Movement for Justice
By Marc Jacobson

When our days become dreary with low-hovering clouds of despair, and when our nights become darker than a thousand midnights, let us remember that there is a creative force in this universe, working to pull down the gigantic mountains of evil, a power that is able to make a way out of no way and transform dark yesterdays into bright tomorrows. Let us realize the arc of the moral universe is long but it bends toward justice.

Rev. Martin Luther King, Jr.

Millions of people work in factories producing clothes for the world. These factories are in Guatemala and China. They are in Los Angeles and Bangladesh. Almost all of them are sweatshops. Wherever workers have no power and limited skills you can find garment sweatshops. It is the leading edge of the dark side of globalization.

In the early 1990's, spurred by free trade agreements that made it easier to import garments into the United States, companies closed up their U.S. factories and re-opened them abroad. The factories opened up wherever labor was cheap and workers were unable to organize. Some of the factories that remained in the United States ignored U.S. labor law and employed migrant workers who did not know their rights and were unlikely to call attention to their miserable wages and working conditions.

As Secretary of Labor under President Clinton, Robert Reich began investigating these workplace abuses and brought some of them to light. When Kathy Lee Gifford acknowledged publicly in 1996 that her clothing brand, sold at Wal-Mart, was made by children in sweatshops in Honduras, the issue came to wide public attention.[1]

In the fall of 1997, some students at Duke University took it upon themselves to ask their university to ensure that all clothing with the Duke logo on it was not made in sweatshops.[2] Their efforts quickly inspired students at other colleges and universities to follow their example. In 1998 student activists launched United Students Against Sweatshops to bring the various campus groups together. The students quickly discovered that they needed a way to monitor whether companies that manufactured their school sweatshirts were in fact living up to their commitment to not use sweatshop labor. So in 2000 the students worked with labor experts and university administrators to form the Workers Rights Consortium.[3]

It did not take long for word of what was happening on campus to inspire people in cities across the country to see if local governments could do what universities were doing. Community members from Maine, New York, Wisconsin and elsewhere got local ordinances passed that required cities to make sure that taxpayer bought clothing was not made in sweatshops. In 2003 these various community activists got together to form a national network that they called SweatFree Communities.[4]

In October 2005 two parents, J and Allison Weiss, were looking to buy school uniforms for their children. They knew that many of the clothes out there were made in sweatshops, and they did not want to buy clothes for their children that were made by other children. J worked for a technology company and Allison took care of their kids full-time. They were an ordinary couple who just wondered what role they were playing in the global economy. They searched on-line and came across the web page for SweatFree Communities. They called and talked to the National Organizer, Liana Foxvog. Liana told them that there was nobody working directly on this issue in Texas, but, fortuitously, Liana had interned for a group called the Texas Fair Trade Coalition that might be interested in helping J and Allison get something going. When they approached Texas Fair Trade Coalition Director Lesley Ramsey, she was interested in the idea. She knew, however, that no city – or university – had yet enacted a sweatfree policy in Texas and it was not clear that it was possible. Nonetheless, they set about reaching out to community leaders and activists. Lesley used her wide network to put out the call, and in January 2006, the Texas Fair Trade Coalition hosted an initial call-to-action meeting to explain the vision for passing an Austin sweatfree ordinance.

Through a power point presentation, J explained that since the success of the universities in developing sweatfree policies a number of cities had followed suit. The city of Los Angeles had passed an ordinance. Los Angeles had even contracted with the Workers Rights Consortium to investigate complaints that arose from the factory floors and to negotiate with the contractors to get workplace abuses fixed.

J alternated between a detailed review of the cities that had passed policies and a passionate plea for Austin to take up the mantle of human rights and economic justice. He had done a little digging and discovered what the city was currently spending on clothing purchases. To the diverse crowd of activists in attendance, J made a special plea for the religious community to get involved. He explained how "religious organizations have played a critical role in passing ethical procurement policies nationally and globally." He pointed out that they were going to be asking the city of Austin to make a values decision in how it purchased goods – and who better to make a case for the values of economic justice and human dignity than the faith community.

At the end of that first meeting, the Austin SweatFree Campaign was launched. One of the first steps was engaging community groups, including religious congregations, to be leaders in the fight. Sean

McGuire, pastoral associate at St. Ignatius Catholic Church, invited the Texas Fair Trade Coalition and a local worker rights group – the Workers Defense Project – to do a presentation and discussion with members of the parish. They discussed the plight of workers in Austin and the plight of workers in sweatshops around the world. They looked at what could be done. The members in attendance decided that a sweatfree ordinance was exactly what was needed. They got approval from the church leadership to endorse the campaign, and signed up to take action when needed.

Rev. Tom Vandestadt was one of two people in attendance at the first meeting who was with a group called the Religion and Labor Network of Austin, also known as RLNA. Rev. Vandestadt was pastor at the Congregational Church of Austin and was an active member of RLNA, at one point serving as co-chair of the organization. Most of RLNA's activities focused on supporting local worker rights struggles, such as when they held a vigil in front of the house of a contractor who repeatedly failed to pay his construction workers for all the hours they had worked.

The RLNA Board discussed the sweatfree campaign and decided to take it on as one of its projects. Rev. Vandestadt argued that it was a great way to engage members of the religious community who had not yet become involved in their other work. So the Board assigned him to be the point person for RLNA on this issue. He and the RLNA Executive Director, Carla Cheatham, quickly stepped in and took a leadership role in the campaign.

At St. Austin's Catholic Church, it was a lay leader who got the parish involved. Ana Frelih-Larsen was an active member of the church's Social Justice Ministry. She had also volunteered in the past for the Texas Fair Trade Coalition. When she heard about the sweatfree campaign, she jumped on board. St. Austin's had an active Just Faith program where parishioners met weekly over a period of months to discuss social justice issues. Ana presented the campaign to this group and they agreed to support it any way they could.

SweatFree Campaign leaders spent just over a year doing presentations and having discussions with groups across the city. At the end, twenty-four organizations had endorsed the effort to pass a sweatfree ordinance. This list included other faith-based groups, community organizations, labor unions, student groups, and fair trade businesses. Representatives of some of these groups and other concerned individuals took a leadership role in the Austin SweatFree Campaign. One or two had a lot of political experience but most had never been involved in anything like this before.

While the campaign was outreaching to different groups, a sub-committee worked on drafting the ordinance by drawing from the best of what other cities had already done. By February 2007 the ordinance was drafted, a strong coalition had been built, and campaign leaders felt ready to start talking to city council members. The first order of business was to determine which city council member they wanted to be the ordinance champion. This champion would have to be super enthusiastic and be willing to do what it took to push the ordinance through the various hoops required to get an ordinance approved by the council.

Campaign members pooled their knowledge of city politics and decided to approach council member Mike Martinez. Martinez had been a firefighter and a member of the firefighters union. He was known as a friend to labor issues, and also as concerned about issues affecting his fellow Latinos. So a SweatFree Campaign delegation comprised of a union member, a faith leader, a member of the ordinance drafting committee, and a Latino community leader went to meet with council member Martinez. His support was immediate and went beyond the expectations of campaign leaders. He agreed to champion the ordinance, and suggested expanding it down the road to include items beyond clothing.

After that first meeting, campaign members worked to set up meetings with the other five city council members. They also approached the Mayor but were told that he would probably go along with whatever the majority of the city council decided. For each city council member, campaign leaders tried to send delegations that included someone from the religious community. The main argument they made to the city council was the moral imperative of the city taking a stand on the abuses of worker dignity that were definitely taking place. City taxpayer dollars were going to buy clothes from factories where workers worked in degrading and dehumanizing conditions, where children worked 80-hour weeks instead of going to school, and where workers were paid wages that did not allow them to adequately feed their families. Campaign leaders knew that this argument had the most resonance coming from faith leaders whose concerns were values-based.

The meetings with city council members went well. Council member Martinez arranged for a city council subcommittee, the Committee on Minority and Women-Owned Business Enterprises, to receive a presentation on the sweatfree ordinance. Representatives from most of the organizations endorsing the Austin SweatFree Campaign attended – at least 25 people in all. It took place on Tuesday afternoon, March 27, 2007. Campaign members had already met with each of the 3 council members on the committee, but this hearing was necessary before the full council could make a decision on the ordinance. Rev. Tom Vandestadt spoke on behalf of the group. He explained the purpose of the ordinance, how it would work, and why it was necessary. He described some of the worker abuses that had been documented at factories doing business with current city contractors. He ended with an impassioned plea for economic justice and for the city to be true to its values of democracy and human rights. The city council committee agreed to bring the issue before the full city council.

Council member Martinez then took the ordinance drafted by the sweatfree campaign and sent it to the city's legal department for review. And there it sat – for months. To help build up the public support needed to push things along, campaign leaders decided to hold film showings to re-energize supporters and get people ready to send e-mails and make phone calls to council members. Ana Frelih-Larsen worked with the Just Faith group to present a showing of the film *China Blue* at St. Austin's. Ana invited Marc Jacobson, who had replaced Lesley Ramsey as Director of the Texas Fair Trade Coalition, to lead a discussion following the film. More than 30 people from various Catholic parishes attended and signed up to take action.

One of the attendees was Barbara Budde, who was Director of Social Ministries for the Catholic Diocese of Austin. She was so energized by the enthusiasm bubbling up from church members across the city that she took it upon herself to present the issue to Bishop Aymond and ask for his support.

A week after the event at St. Austin's, Rev. Vandestadt hosted a film showing – also of *China Blue* – at his church. Rev. Vandestadt, working with other campaign leaders from student and community groups, sent out a general invitation. More than 80 people packed into the church sanctuary to watch the film and learn about the sweatfree campaign.

The Religion and Labor Network, seeing the positive response to the faith community voice but knowing that more support was necessary to push the ordinance through, decided to create a list of clergy endorsers. Carla Cheatham, RLNA's Executive Director, sent out a message to their clergy list and spoke with prominent clergy in the city to galvanize their support. By June, that list had grown to more than 20 clergy. It included Methodists, Lutherans, Church of Christ, Catholics, Baptists, Quakers, and Presbyterians. In the middle of June, Council member Martinez finally sent word that the ordinance was ready and the full council would vote on it. The council vote was set for June 21, 2007.

Campaign members had not encountered any significant opposition in their meetings with city council members, but there were enough questions raised that they were not sure of the final vote tally. A couple of council members had raised questions about funding. They were told that the sweatfree campaign was asking for the city to set aside funds equaling 1% of city garment purchases to use to hire an independent monitoring agency. SweatFree Communities was in the process of setting up a State and Local SweatFree Consortium, modeled after the universities' Workers Rights Consortium, to coordinate that monitoring. And, in all likelihood, that is what the city would be asked to join.

Council members also asked if the city would end up paying more for clothing because of the new requirements. The city of Austin's procurement director, Byron Johnson, who had contacted other cities to inquire about their ordinances, learned that there had been no significant increase in the prices charged to cities for garment contracts.

In the week leading up to the city council meeting, campaign members put the word out to all those who had signed up to support the campaign that now was the time to make their voices heard. Dozens of people sent e-mails to their council members. Others prepared to be there at 9 a.m. for the vote. Bishop Aymond sent a letter to each of the council members asking for his/her support. The Austin American-

Statesman interviewed campaign members and council member Martinez for an article about the impending decision.

When SweatFree Campaign supporters arrived on the morning of the vote, they were told that there was no need for any further presentation. After the council convened, it first approved the hiring of a new police commissioner. Then it took up the sweatfree ordinance. The first council member to comment was council member Mike Martinez. He applauded the members of the Austin SweatFree Campaign for their efforts, and encouraged the council to support this worthy endeavor. Another council member, Lee Leffingwell, spoke in support of the ordinance. Then council member Sheryl Cole spoke about how important it was for the city to stand up for human rights, and said how impressed she was by the amount of support for the ordinance coming out of the religious community. The vote was unanimous. The city of Austin passed a sweatfree ordinance, becoming the first city in Texas to do so.

What began with two parents inquiring into their children's clothing galvanized community and faith leaders across the city of Austin and led to a city ordinance. But it did not end there. That same coalition went on to get Travis County, in which Austin resides, to pass a sweatfree policy. People in other Texas cities heard about Austin's success and began their own sweatfree campaigns. Jim Hightower, a prominent Texas activist, posted a story on his national newsletter, and some activists in Arizona were inspired to start a sweatfree campaign there also. And so the sweatfree movement continued to grow.

Notes

[1] http://www.prospect.org/cs/articles?article=the_campus_antisweatshop_movement.
[2] Ibid.
[3] USAS web page: http://www.studentsagainstsweatshops.org/index.php?option=com_content&task=view&id=21&Itemid=50.
[4] http://www.sweatfree.org/about_us.

About the Author

Marc Jacobson served as Director of the Texas Fair Trade Coalition from 2006 to 2008. Prior to that, he did faith-based and neighborhood organizing in Texas, California, and Massachusetts. He holds a Master of Public Policy from the John F. Kennedy School of Government at Harvard University.

People Power!
By Larry James

Moving from pastoral, parish ministry after almost twenty-five years to manage and develop an inner-city poverty relief organization provided numerous and instantaneous opportunities for reflection, self-doubt and experimentation! When I made this move at mid-life, I was certain that I knew what Jesus said about poverty, injustice and those caught up in and crushed by both. Beyond my clear theology of liberation and my hope for the realization of justice, I didn't know much else! However, when you honestly don't know what to do to more effectively and practically pursue your mission, you find yourself falling back on faith, openness to surprising new ideas, and "a clear word from the Lord."

Let me attempt an explanation. Without a doubt this concept or better, this understanding is the most important truth I have learned over the past fifteen years: ***People possess the power, the capacity and the desire to solve their own problems, if they are given the resources they need and the opportunities they crave.***

People don't need *help* nearly as much as they need a *chance*. I bump into this reality every day. Years ago, my role at **Central Dallas Ministries** was much different than it is today. The freedom I enjoy to lead in different directions today is due largely to the wisdom and the power of the people with whom I work. When I arrived in 1994, I was spending five days a week interviewing low-income people in our Food Pantry. I helped stock food shelves. I drove our delivery truck. I advocated for clients with other agencies. On Sundays, I was out in churches begging for money and volunteers. Frankly, I wasn't doing very well on either count because we were always short of both!

Back then, all of our volunteers drove in from affluent suburban churches and neighborhoods. Everyone who volunteered was white. All of the material resources were on one side of the equation we had created. All of the perceived need was on the other. Relationships with the community and its people always felt pretty much "one down." Our approach had become totally charity-based, paternalistic, and neo-colonial. I knew that we were on the wrong track with our noble efforts, but I didn't really know what to do to correct our process.

One day my world and the world of CDM changed in a moment. I found myself facing three Hispanic mothers with their beautiful children. The three women were perfect strangers to one another and to me. Our little group approach I am certain was not a very "professional" way to do "social work." But then, I've never had a social work class in my life. These three delightful women were attempting to combine their limited English to overcome my inability to speak Spanish. They weren't getting too far in informing me about their challenges.

As we sat there in growing frustration, **Josefina Ortiz**, an older woman who had already been interviewed and assisted, walked by. I stopped her and asked if she could help me. I learned then, and have learned many times since, that this is a very important question for "helpers" to learn how to ask those they seek to "help." She replied that she would be very happy to help me. She sat down with us and translated the conversation. As a result, we were able to provide the assistance the three families sought. As they were leaving, I turned to Ms. Ortiz and began thanking her profusely, still not realizing what an asset I had right in front of me. When she reached the door to leave our center, Josefina had the good sense to turn back to me. I will never forget what she said: "*Larry, I could come back tomorrow and help you.*" I told her that would be great because, as she could see, I needed the help! Josefina came back "tomorrow" for nine years.

That afternoon when the pantry closed, I returned to my upstairs office. As I was looking out my large window on the "crack house" next door, I received a very clear message from God's heart. The message was in two parts. First, I was told that I was dead wrong about the neighborhood. Even though I thought I knew what it needed, I couldn't possibly know. Second, I had been wrong to look at the community only in terms of *need*, especially material need as I and others had defined and limited that need. Rather, I should look at the neighborhood in terms of its *assets*. And, I should realize that there are all kinds of assets besides the material variety.

Immediately, Josefina's face came to mind. The lesson was so clear. The truth so obvious. Over the next forty-five days we set out to change our organizational culture and change it quickly. Every person who came through our doors was encouraged to talk not just about their needs, but also about their assets. Further, we invited every person who came to us to return and serve the community as a volunteer. Almost overnight we had more volunteers than we knew what to do with.

Several things happened. We lost almost all of our suburban volunteers. We now have several hundred volunteers in our database and 99% are community people who continue to access our various resources and services. People from outside the community who were our supporters questioned our sanity. "*Looks like you have the lunatics running the asylum,*" one dedicated supporter told me with a smile. "*These people will steal you blind,*" I was told in countless ways, again and again. Finally, I had the presence of mind to form a standard reply that went something like, "*You know, you are correct. In this business you're going to have some theft. But, I've noticed that it is one of two kinds. It's either canned corn or human dignity. I'm going with the canned corn cartel!*"

Over the years we've stayed with this model. *It is the one essential, fixed, non-negotiable ingredient in our mix here at CDM.* Whatever success we have enjoyed is directly related to this approach and to the principle of "people power" back of it. This amazing group of people (continually changing, ever open to new members) serves as a 24-7 "think tank" of sorts. Every idea, every initiative, every response to poverty that we have undertaken across the years has arisen from the collective and individual wisdom expressed by these amazing people.

Today, Central Dallas Ministries provides emergency assistance to families in need, community-based health care services, a public interest law firm with legal representation on behalf of the voiceless, workforce training, technology education, high quality experiential after school programming, leadership and community organizing skill development, affordable housing for the working poor and homeless, counseling services, comprehensive engagement with youth who "age out" of the foster care system in our state, free nutritious lunch program for over 7,000 children throughout the summer months, a large and aggressive AmeriCorps team serving all across our region, scholarship opportunities for urban youth, resale businesses and a number of additional initiatives designed to strengthen and build community in inner city Dallas.

Every idea, every effort, every endeavor has sprung to life thanks to the wisdom and vision of "the poor" people with whom we work. There is no way for me to overestimate their importance or their continuing impact. Talk about wealth! Social capital and collective efficacy continue to transform everything about our efforts to re-invent and develop community in inner-city neighborhoods here in Dallas, Austin and San Antonio where we have planted sister organizations. Many of our programs are staffed and led by the very people we initially sought to "serve" as a rather traditional charity. But we've moved far beyond charity to community engagement and solidarity with the people. The people provide the genius behind our work.

Mark it down. If your mission is to grow community and stand with individuals, families and neighborhoods ravaged by the unforgiving, cruel forces of poverty as they engage their own power, then ...

- People cannot be treated as projects.
- People cannot be treated as problems.
- People cannot be treated as if they should be disconnected or disengaged from the primary process at work.
- People must not be seen as clients.
- People must be trusted and valued as they are, for who they are.

You see, transforming truth is quite different. The truth is, people are my neighbors and I am their neighbor. The truth is, people–all people–are powerful. The truth is, people are beautiful, promising, full of wonder and great, great potential.

Because of our relationship with the people of the communities where we live and work, we've developed a clear philosophy that guides our work. Included in our operational strategy are the following principles or core understandings that guide us as we pursue our mission. Again, each value proposition comes to us from the community itself and from our experiences among the people –

- We believe in the ability of people to solve their own problems when given access to opportunity and resources.
- We believe the resources within a community are adequate to initiate genuine renewal and redevelopment.
- We devote ourselves to the discovery and mobilization of individual and community resources and capacities.
- We believe in partnership and collaboration, therefore we hold all of the resources at our disposal with an open hand.
- We believe racial reconciliation is a prerequisite for genuine community renewal.
- We believe that our walk with God will always lead us into the community around us.
- We believe "re-neighboring" will be an important part of community development and renewal, and as a result many of us now live in the inner city alongside our friends and neighbors.
- We believe charity must be replaced by compassionate community building as a basic strategy.
- We believe that for community to thrive the institutions that make genuine community possible must be respected and renewed, including homes, schools, faith communities, labor and health and wellness organizations.
- We believe the public, private and faith-based organizations of a city must all play important roles in community redevelopment.
- We believe it better to teach a man to fish rather than to give him a fish, but best of all is "pond ownership."
- We believe in the value of both chaos and ownership. Chaos, or what's faith for? And ownership, because if the people don't own the work, we are clearly on the wrong track!

People power--it is the only place to start, to live, to conclude.

About the author

Larry M. James serves as the leadership executive for Central Dallas Ministries, a faith-based corporation working in several inner city neighborhoods in Dallas and San Antonio, Texas. Beginning as a small food pantry, Central Dallas Ministries has grown dramatically and developed innovative human and community development designed to benefit and provide hopeful opportunity to thousands who experience the challenges and the barriers presented by poverty.

The Reformation of Compassion
By Michael Piazza

For much of the two decades I have served as one of the leaders of the Cathedral of Hope, the church has been known as the largest predominantly lesbian and gay congregation in the world. Recently, with our inclusion into the United Church of Christ, that identity has shifted a bit, and we have become known as the only liberal mega-church in the South. Both of these identities have seemed at times to be oxymorons for a community of faith in Dallas, Texas.

When I arrived in this bastion of conservative politics and religion in 1987, the two issues that challenged our congregation most were homophobia and HIV/AIDS. This was a city and a state where discrimination against lesbian, gay, bisexual and transgender (LGBT) people was the norm. In addition, the AIDS epidemic was killing a tragic number of young men here. Many churches refused to care for the sick and dying, some funeral homes refused to accept their bodies, and medical care was difficult to find and often required long hours of waiting at the public hospital.

Today, Dallas is a very different city around these issues. Out lesbian and gay people hold high elected offices, and the level of care for persons with HIV/AIDS is among the best in the country. It is my conviction that the prophetic ministry of the Cathedral of Hope made a significant contribution to that transformation. However, it might not have been in the ways you imagined. Oh, to be sure, we protested and marched and held press conferences. We signed petitions and wrote letters and made phone calls. Those things certainly made a difference, but the church's greatest contribution may have come through a different strategy.

A case could be made that Dallas is one of the cities in America that is most divided by class and economic status. The school system is composed almost entirely of children of color. The city is largely, though not completely, divided, with people of color living in the south and the white, middle and upper classes living north of downtown. The Trinity River often is referred to casually as the dividing line, and the absence of outrage about this is startling. It forces one to check the calendar and make sure that 20 years really have passed ... or maybe even 40.

While it was tempting for this congregation to decide that economic issues were not their primary concern, we simply could not ignore the overwhelming witness of the gospels and prophets. It was a quote by Mother Teresa that focused our minds and became the prophetic word for our calling: "Too many words. Let them just see what we do." Although our primary identity hasn't shifted, the major thrust of our resources and energy has. For the past decade, the congregation has given away more than $1 million in money, resources and services to the poor and those in need.

This ministry, which is generally referred to as Community Outreach, has maintained many classic programs, and initiated some rather ambitious projects. By mobilizing both money and volunteers, we literally built a school for AIDS orphans in the Dominican Republic. We have constructed a series of buildings for a very poor community in Reynosa, Mexico, and now the people of that community are assisting their neighbors. We have partnered with Habitat for Humanity and worked with People Helping People, a program of the City of Dallas, to renovate dozens of homes for the elderly poor who faced eviction because their homes failed to meet occupancy standards.

Our congregation collects food and has its own food pantry, though most of the food goes to support various food banks. We also host hundreds of homeless for a sit-down breakfast every Saturday morning. Recently, the members of one of the church's ministries tried to sign up to lead this project one morning and were told there was a waiting list of volunteers. All of these programs are supported by a staff member and a team of incredibly devoted volunteers. They have created their own management team with very little oversight or even input from church leaders or staff. These, and dozens of other projects, are supported by a multitude of volunteers, whom we call ministers. Now that may seem like a nice idea, but it is actually the core of why this ministry works. In fact, let me tell you two factors for its success and two unexpected results.

First, the groundwork was laid by prophetic preaching that created a shift in the values of a community that can be as selfish and classist as any. We challenged people to recognize Jesus' teaching that if God had any favorites it was the poor. In a culture where the wealthy are held up as heroes, we literally named as saints those who have given their resources and lives to care for "the least." Creating this shift in values required us to be direct, relentless and persistent. We used every means available to recognize those who had chosen to heed Mother Teresa's advice and stopped talking about their faith and started living it out. It was critical, especially at the outset, that the pastors and other leaders be among those who incarnated this theology and value. It also was critical that we be seen as assisting not leading. We literally sought to give the ministry away. While it is often easier for staff to simply "do it themselves," it was not acceptable for staff to take ministry away from the people.

And that is the other factor for this amazing shift. Our congregation comes from almost every denomination. About 25 percent are Roman Catholic, and about 25 percent are Southern Baptist. The rest are a diverse gathering. This is the perfect formula for division and conflict. In our tradition, creeds are considered testimonies, not tests of faith, so we have been forced to discover what it uniquely means to be a member of our congregation. For almost two decades, I taught only a very small portion of our confirmation/membership class. The part I taught consisted of telling them that, while they were more than welcome to "hang out" with us, becoming a member of the church had a specific meaning.

After outgrowing two facilities, our church, for many years, has had multiple services while still experiencing overflow crowds. One thing we really didn't need was simply more members. We needed more ministers. We went on to tell persons that they were too gifted to simply hold down our pews and that my job as the pastor was to equip them to use their gifts to build up the body of Christ (Ephesians 4:12-13). Being a minister means you have decided to take off your bib and put on your apron; to go from being a guest in the house of the Lord to being a host.

We begin each worship service by welcoming our guests and telling them that the people sitting around them are the ministers of the church.

We end each worship hour by reminding them that "our worship has ended, but NOW our service begins." We commission them as the Body of Christ to go into the world and serve. In the structure of the church, we have sought to minimize management and maximize ministry. In short, we have tried to create a comprehensive, compelling culture of service to the poor, the excluded, the marginalized and the oppressed.

The result of our success in this shift in life values and vision has been surprising even to me. First, we discovered that who we were and how we served beyond our local church dramatically transformed how we were seen and understood by the larger community. For years, we had tried to convince people that LGBT folks also could be Christian. Our Biblical and theological arguments met with limited results, but our witness as a compassionate community powerfully transformed how others understood lesbian and gay people. After many years of wanting to be in relationship with the largely Hispanic neighborhood adjoining the church, we discovered that helping their children's schools convinced them that our witness was valid. One of our associate pastors overheard a conversation in a local restaurant in which two older men had just read an article about some service project we had undertaken. One of the men was heard to say, "I'm still not sure about this homosexual stuff, but I sure wish our church was half as Christian as theirs is."

The other startling result was the transformation of our own congregation. I know it should be painfully obvious, but it took me a while to discover that, if you want to feel good about yourself, be a good person. All of the therapy in the world didn't have the power to transform a historically oppressed and rejected people as much as simply allowing them to be the kind and compassionate people they really are. It is my belief that a mirror is a powerful tool for a pastor or a leader, so long as you know which side to use. We tried to hold up a mirror to a community that was making a difference. Almost weekly, we showed them images and told them stories of the ways their devotion and sacrifice were making a difference. After years of arguing with family, the larger church and society that lesbian and gay people were daughters and sons of God, this congregation saw with their own eyes proof positive.

Seeing themselves and their fellow parishioners being the kind of people they always thought Christians should be was a transforming experience. No longer did they hear the Hebrew prophet's words as a rebuke, but they shared the prophet's conviction that caring for the poor was the call of God.

For most of our lives, lesbian and gay people have been excluded from the Church. Even though more and more congregations are welcoming, mainline denominations, with few exceptions, still do not ordain or marry openly gay or lesbian members. No other people are simply categorically refused those rites. As a result, no amount of hospitality can erase the fact that the Church still does not regard lesbian, gay, bisexual and transgender people as being fully and truly Christian. How do you undo the impact of centuries of inferiorization in the name of God? How do you create an antidote to the historical witness of the church and change society's view of LGBT people? Shortly after I arrived at the Cathedral of Hope the congregation adopted as two of its goals to be changing the way much of the world thinks about lesbian and gay people and changing what many lesbian and gay people think about God. Many strategic approaches might have been taken. While I cannot claim that I was wise enough to know that mobilizing thousands of people to care for those in need would accomplish those two goals, it has been one of the greatest serendipities of my ministry.

About the author

Rev. Michael S. Piazza is a spiritual visionary, author and social justice advocate who currently serves as Dean of the Cathedral of Hope, a congregation of the United Church of Christ. He also serves as president of Hope for Peace and Justice, a non-profit ministry of Cathedral of Hope whose mission is equipping progressive people of faith to be champions for peace and justice.

Asylum for Central Americans and
Justice through Sister Church Covenants
By Gail Smith

How do we balance church projects involving charity toward our poor neighbors and seeking justice for the poor? Over the years our sister church relationship with Maria Madre de los Pobres (Mary Mother of the Poor) parish in San Salvador, has fallen in both the justice end and the middle part of the spectrum spanning acts of justice and acts of charity. We began our project as a search for justice by advocating the ending of U.S. support for an unjust civil war in El Salvador. From the beginning we provided some financial support for Maria Madre's general church budget. More recently, at the parish's request, we provided financial assistance for 24 of their school-age children.

We sustained our justice work by providing consciousness-raising education for our local church members. For example, along with other local churches we sponsored resolutions designed to move the national leadership of The United Methodist Church towards using its influence nationally to modify U.S. foreign policy in the Cold War, as well as provide fair asylum policies for undocumented immigrants.

The work brought us new church friends from here and abroad. However, long-term maintenance of support has depended on charitable activities closer to the other end of the spectrum of mission work. We found that church members interested in joining more conventional mission trips centered on short term work projects were reluctant to travel with a mission team interested in deepening church relationships based on shared life experiences or "accompaniment." Later, our members became more interested in visiting Maria Madre when that mission trip included visiting specific children for whom we helped provide educational support.

In the decades of the 80's and 90's, thousands of Salvadoran immigrants moved into our local Dallas/Ft. Worth area. They were not readily accepted into the dominantly Mexican Latino communities in our area. All were competing for jobs to sustain their families, but many of these newer immigrants were also seeking to remain legally in our country under asylum protection. Many of us came to understand that U.S. policy towards El Salvador was one of the factors driving the huge increase in undocumented immigrants from Central America entering the U.S. illegally. Our country's cold-war policy also drove the rejection of nearly all these asylum claims.

Many of our church members' experience in the 60's and 70's helped us understand the issues associated with illegal immigration in the 80's. We had joined citywide efforts to combat racism by joining civil rights demonstrations and consciousness raising courses focusing on institutional racism and institutional sexism. So by the time the decade of the 80's began, several of our church members were experienced in using the joint actions of our Outreach Commission, our adult Sunday school classes, and our Administrative Board's power to authorize actions. In addition, we relied on several members' volunteer experiences in local non-profit organizations to personalize and localize church interest in acting on the dire plight of undocumented asylum seeking refugees in the Dallas area.

Early on our Sunday school class read and discussed the history of Liberation Theology that advocates political action based on belief in God's preferential option for the poor. Our study of what happens to the marginalized people of this world, and specifically those persons living south of our border, resonated with me. My participation in the women's movement, my graduate education, and subsequent full-time employment in the public school system, helped me realize how brainwashed I had been as a girl and woman growing up in a sexist culture. I approached the issues surrounding granting asylum in the US for Central Americans through my own experience of limitations imposed by white male dominated power structures in churches and schools, and by unequal practices dictated through public policy, consumer credit law, and family law. Church-sponsored projects focusing on civil rights make sense in the context of liberation theology. Or, more traditional Bible study of Jesus' teachings focusing on who is our neighbor or the acts of a Good Samaritan provide obvious contexts for these projects. Even children's Sunday school classes singing "Jesus loves me this I know, for the Bible tells me so ..." make good lessons for all of us. The hymn does not say: "Jesus loves me more if I'm a white, straight male, middle class, U.S. citizen."

Of course most of us have never experienced the undocumented workers' fears, dangers, and hardships while fleeing across countries, crossing illegally over borders, or eking out a meager living by taking on day work in restaurants, individual homes and gardens, factories, or construction sites. But it was easy to overlook their lives here in the U.S. because we had officially marginalized their situation. Our government treated them as part of the greater cold war dividing the world into communist and capitalist spheres of influence. According to our government's narrative, the good capitalist, democratic government of El Salvador was fighting a war against indigenous peasants who were mostly Marxist guerillas; therefore, Salvadoran refugees fleeing the civil war in El Salvador were Marxist enemies of the US. I learned what this meant in human terms through my volunteer work on the board of a nonprofit organization providing legal representation for asylum in Dallas immigration courts. Virtually no one was granted asylum no matter how well documented were claims of certain death if deported to El Salvador.

We came to believe that justice for these people was important, not only in political and human rights terms, but also in theological terms. These concerns were shared among members of our Outreach Commission. Our Sunday school class and the Outreach Commission agreed to sponsor a series of interviews and speakers and a course on the political history of El Salvador and Central America for Sunday morning and evening programs. We learned how other churches, a few in Dallas and others in Arizona, were offering sanctuary to Salvadoran refugees and heard speakers from the three churches in Dallas who were participating in the sanctuary movement. We met the first Salvadoran family members chosen by the Dallas sanctuary movement who were met by their sanctuary church members soon after crossing into Texas illegally and were transported to Dallas to live in a Catholic church.

I hoped our Outreach Commission would sponsor a resolution to our Administrative Board making us a sanctuary church; however, some members of the commission argued that such an action would make the church liable for damaging consequences by breaking U.S. immigration law. Others believed the sanctuary movement was too politically divisive and would anger some church members. We compromised by bringing a resolution to the Board supporting our church developing a "sister church relationship" with a congregation in

El Salvador. We wanted to use that relationship as a way of learning more about what was really happening there and what role our government was playing in the Salvadoran civil war.

Financial support for this project was not included in the church's official operating and outreach budget so we agreed to seek funding from our church's extra-budget, second mile giving program, the Human Development Fund. The fact that it would not affect the church budget helped members on the Board approve the resolution. Several opposed the project based on their belief that we might be aiding Marxists and Communists through having a sister church partner in El Salvador. However, we made plans to initiate our project with Sunday school class members who agreed to actively support the sister church relationship.

We were fortunate to know a member of another Dallas area United Methodist church active in the sanctuary movement who had moved to El Salvador to work with a Lutheran church organization conducting study tours in El Salvador for churches and seminaries. She suggested that we partner with a Roman Catholic parish, named Maria Madre de los Pobres (Mary Mother of the Poor), located in the slum outskirts of the capital city of San Salvador. The church was a member of the network of Catholic churches called Base Christian Communities that implemented the insights and teachings of Liberation theologians. Through our friend's mediation, Maria Madre agreed to the partnership. Representatives of two Dallas area United Methodist churches visited the Maria Madre Catholic parish in San Salvador in March 1988. Thus we became a three-way sister partnership consisting of two Dallas United Methodist churches and one Salvadoran Roman Catholic church.

Our two Dallas area churches organized the visit as a fact finding/ educational delegation, rather than a more typical church mission trip. This was our introduction to a very crucial insight about church mission work. In contrast to several generations ago, I believe most church mission trips reflect the truism that you can feed a hungry person for a day if you give him or her a fish, but you can feed that person for a lifetime if you teach him or her to fish. Many groups participating in mission trips understand their work to be much more than evangelizing on behalf of Christianity. Today, mission work often focuses on joint projects between host and visiting churches that improve the lives of poor people. However, we can lose sight of the fact that most all the poor and/or marginalized people of the world are restricted to fishing in waters severely depleted of fish. If we do not address these "fishing restrictions," learning how to fish will rarely result in having enough fish to eat. In terms of this metaphor, we traveled to El Salvador specifically to meet the priest and lay leaders of Maria Madre de los Pobres parish in order to understand what kinds of fishing restrictions they faced.

We learned their restrictions were complex and included not only extreme lack of income, but lack of city services including water, sewer, electricity, paved roads, free public schools, and affordable health care. They lacked access to legal representation and police protection, and were inflicted with constant hostile surveillance in their neighborhood by government police and military forces. Their own conservative Catholic Church hierarchy and the Vatican in Rome provided little if any protection from death threats to laity and clergy from paramilitary death squads. Their most recent crisis was the abduction/arrest by the military or police (no one was sure which) of one of their church's catechists (we would call him a Sunday-school teacher.). He had been preparing children for Easter services at an affiliated church in a more rural area outside of the city. Our delegation's first meeting with the priest and lay members of Maria Madre took place in front of a military jail where they waited for their priest to meet with the jail staff to find out if this was the jail in which their lay catechist was incarcerated.

The power of what it means to "accompany" or "be in solidarity with" our sister church was obvious. They needed our presence, the presence of U.S. citizens, to provide some safety for their search. Arresting U.S. citizens would cause unwanted publicity and scrutiny of government treatment of church members who worked with the poorest citizens in El Salvador. We joined their search traveling across the city from jail to military base to jail as late evening dusk turned into dark night. Finally, at our last stop, some of our delegation joined the priest when he entered a jail to face the authorities. His people were very afraid he would be detained without our presence.

Jail officials admitted to holding our young man and insisted that he would be held, as usual, for 72 hours without having access to outside representation. Fearing his torture in the jail, we returned to our hotel to make calls back home to our pastors and to our congressional representatives asking them to send word to the U.S. Embassy in San Salvador, the Salvadoran President, and U.S. government officials in Washington D.C. denouncing the arrest of the catechist by attesting he was not a Marxist member of the armed guerilla forces in the rural countryside. We were able to personalize human rights abuses through asking church members to make phone calls and send letters to government officials. At the end of our week's visit, we joyfully participated in the parish celebration of his release from jail and his presence leading the parish children in their Palm Sunday procession through their neighborhood. Our churches shared this period of worry, fear, frustration and joy. Our experience formed a bond lasting over 20 years.

How can a mission project be sustained over a long time period? The answer is – not easily – and certainly not evenly over 20 plus years. We returned from our first mission trip inspired to tell as many people as possible about conditions in El Salvador and the role of U.S. policy and U.S. military in supporting continuing civil rights abuses and violence on the vast majority of Salvadoran citizens. We formed a United Methodist church committee to compose resolutions against U.S. foreign policy in El Salvador for adoption by our area church conference. We handed out plain black crocheted crosses to our church members and every one who attended The United Methodist North Texas Annual Conference in 1988. Over 20 years later, one of my church friends told me that same small black cross still serves her as a reminder of our sister church relationship with Maria Madre.

We have learned that it is important to find concrete symbols depicting the more abstract goals of social justice. For a second example, on the first visit we took some of our church banners to present to the parish during its worship service, and we later received a banner made especially for us by women in their church. We also received one of the distinctive wooden Salvadoran crosses depicting rural peasant community life. It remains on display in our sanctuary as a reminder of our common redemptive community with the poor in the world and especially the poor in our Salvadoran sister parish.

Our sister church members are facing similar challenges sustaining work for justice in their Salvadoran community. Along with providing health care and educational services in their parish, they stress the importance of creating ceremonies and sites that commemorate martyrs for justice in the civil war. Our joint participation in these commemorative occasions is an important means of keeping our sisterhood alive over so many years. When we attend mass there, our Protestant members have been invited to carry the host elements and take communion in their Catholic mass. Some of us have attended weddings and high school graduations there. Our pastors and priests have spoken in each other's worship services. Thus personal visits to each other's churches are crucial means for sustaining our cross-border and cross-denomination family.

Approximately 12 years ago, parish leaders at Maria Madre de los Pobres asked us to sponsor some elementary students in their parish neighborhood. Renewed interest in the project was generated through sponsoring these children. An appeal to our congregation drew about 20 of our families to support 20 of their elementary students. In the second year, more personal interest in these children was generated through having their pictures, reading their school report cards, and exchanging cards and letters. Members wanted to visit the children. Our visit provided a gut wrenching and eye opening experience for our delegation. Although interest in visiting the parish has not been sustained past the first two or three years, our church families have continued to financially participate in the program long enough that many of our children have graduated from high school. Some of us have continued to support them in their first years of college or vocational school. The children's project continues to keep many members interested in what goes on in Maria Madre parish and in US policy towards El Salvador and Central America.

Our project's current focus is educating our congregation about global trade, the Central American Free Trade Association, and effects of these policies on our sister parish in El Salvador and the economy and environment in Texas and Dallas. Members of Maria Madre know a lot more about global poverty and global trade than members of our local United Methodist churches. They have much to teach us about combating violations of human rights, poverty and global warming. We are all called to be good stewards of our earth, and we are called to be seekers of justice and human rights on behalf of all people living on the earth. Our convictions will enable us to find the means to support immigrants living among us and to combat the causes that make it necessary for them to risk their lives to live and work here.

In summary, positive experiences in sustaining work for social justice include:

- Choosing projects that relate to studies in theology.
- Choosing projects in which members of your congregation can relate personally.
- Connecting international projects to local concerns for justice.
- Finding allied churches and organizations to provide support and training.
- Involving several groups within the church's structure to expand interest and responsibility.
- Planning ways to address language barriers and safety issues on mission trips.
- Creating symbols and events that remind the congregation of the project.
- Expecting changes that bring new understandings and rejuvenate interest over many years.

About the author

Gail Smith has been a member of Northaven United Methodist Church in Dallas, Texas for over 40 years. Over the decades, she has participated in church programs focusing on women's consciousness raising, preschool education, institutional racism, immigration reform, and GLBT rights in church and society. Gail worked in educational research in Dallas public schools for 22 years; now retired she continues her church activities along with regular mission trips to accompany our extended church family in El Salvador.

Just the Basics: Food, Shelter, Hope
By Stephen Wiard

My understanding of justice and social action finds its roots in Isaiah 58, Matthew 25 and in the present realities in which I live. The fact is that northern New Mexico, where Taos is located, has one of the highest poverty rates in the nation. Contrast this with Los Alamos County, just a few miles away, which is one of the wealthiest. When nearly 30% of New Mexico children are living in poverty, what's a preacher to do? What's a congregation to do? Read, pray, organize and take action!

For me, the call to ministry is to be found in a relevant and sometimes radical 'social gospel.' I think the institutional church needs to get beyond the status quo if it is truly to be called the Body of Christ and exemplify what progressive Christianity is all about. The weekly exposure to the people who come to us for help has deepened my faith, broadened my socio-economic awareness and humbled me daily.

In order to address the issue of food insecurity, i.e., hunger, the congregation of El Pueblito United Methodist Church made an effort in 1994 to reach out to those in our midst. Several members of the church began serving hot meals to people in the community in a program called "Shared Table." By making food available to those in need, a small church of fifty members made a leap of faith and launched a program that currently, assists approximately 7,000 people a year (5,000 adults and 2,000 children).

Our program has expanded considerably since those early days, from serving hot meals to distributing food commodities and basic health care items twice a month on the second and fourth Wednesdays all year round. Our program differs from those that require participants to fall below certain income requirements. Anyone who needs food may come to the "Table" and we will share what we have. This growth is due partly to ever-increasing need as well as a more inclusive understanding of scripture and the call for social justice/equity among all of God's children.

We also made the decision to help meet other basic needs beyond food. For some time now we have provided items such as soap, shampoo, toothpaste, disposable diapers, tampons, condoms, toilet paper, etc. Emergency assistance for prescription medications is also provided, when funds are available, to those who participate in the Shared Table program.

The congregation of El Pueblito UMC has made the church building available for storage and distribution of goods and services. A local Presbyterian church has allowed us to use their facility on the opposite end of town, which has proven especially helpful to those without reliable transportation.

As the pastor of the church, I also serve as the director of the Shared Table program. There are three part-time staff who assist in the kitchen, i.e., a pantry manager, an assistant, and an individual who drives our van to pick up food in the community from local restaurants and stores.

Several years ago when I was given the opportunity to speak to a local elementary school about the Shared Table, one fourth grader said, "I like the Shared Table because you might not think you need anything, but you just might." This form of community outreach to those who, for whatever reason, find themselves on the margins of society, has given our church a meaningful identity and purpose, both externally and internally.

Another significant example of social action that helped meet a very real need in the community was the establishment of the Taos Men's Shelter, a 12-bed facility for homeless men. Because of the notoriety of Shared Table, many referrals/requests for overnight shelter would be directed to me as Pastor/Director. The community has, for some time, had a shelter for battered women, but no such facility existed for men.

As a result, an organization called Taos Coalition to End Homelessness (TCEH), consisting of several movers and shakers within the community, came together to find a solution to a problem that recurred every winter. The local congregation supported my serving as President of the Coalition's Board. We proceeded to work closely with the Town Council, County Commissioners, and the local school district to meet the needs of homeless men in Taos.

After a lengthy search for a site that was 'suitable' to local skeptics who agreed with the concept but did not support a men's shelter in their neighborhood, the Town Council and the County worked together to allot a parcel of land near the County Courthouse. The school district donated an old mobile-pre-fab classroom building that was then moved to the site and made ready for occupancy through much volunteer labor and in-kind donations from community members.

The men show up in the evening and are provided a hot meal, brought in by community and church volunteers. They are asked to leave the building in the morning. A full-time on-site manager was hired as well as an executive director to help carry out the responsibilities.

While not the hub, our church has been identified by many as a significant spoke in the wheel of progressive Christianity within our community. As we struggle to feed and shelter those on the margins we must be prepared to wrestle with the status quo as we find it within our individual communities. People do not turn to the grocery stores, the banks, the hardware stores, or the local sports bar to assist them in providing food and shelter when they are in need, but they do look to the church in those times.

Therefore, we decided to ask every local church, synagogue, and mosque to take a special offering the weekend before Thanksgiving as a way to help support our local men's shelter. The church is called to be the conscience of the community and, as such, is urged by necessity to respond to the clarion call of the prophetic tradition.

Our experience is that, for the most part, people are willing to help organize or give money to the cause if timely and compassionate leadership is present to guide the process. While working with diverse personalities and city/county agencies and commissions, my experience has taught me to be persistently tactful in pursuing the goal of establishing a men's shelter or a community-wide food pantry. It also involves continuous and sincere efforts that evoke positive public relations. The community needs to hear and to know some of the personal stories that are encountered on a regular basis before the strategy/theory of social justice is able to become a viable program the community will support.

I am continually humbled by the circumstances of our ministry and outreach. The face of God walks through our kitchen door every week. Several years ago, I was preparing for our annual Christmas Eve candlelight/communion service when I heard a knock at the door. A couple with a small child was passing through town on a snowy Christmas Eve and stopped at the church asking for assistance. They asked if I had any bread. I replied that no, we did not have any bread. And then I realized that we did have bread after all, the evening's communion bread. I proceeded to give them half a loaf of the communion bread and bless them on their way.

Perhaps all we can hope for in life is to share some of our bread and remember that two or more roads often provide us a choice on life's journey. May God's spirit and the prophet's call to social justice nudge us onward toward the road that needs more travel ... Happy trails!

About the author

Steve Wiard is currently serving in his twelfth year as pastor of El Pueblito United Methodist Church in Taos, New Mexico, as well as director of the Shared Table. Prior to his time in New Mexico, Steve taught high school social science in Council Grove, Kansas for 18 years and also served three 2-year terms in the Kansas House of Representatives from 1988-1994. He is presently serving as President of the Board of Directors of the New Mexico Conference of Churches.

Questions for Reflection and Discussion

1. What theological beliefs motivated taking on the vocation of justice in these narratives?

2. What connection do you see between these contemporary efforts on behalf of justice and biblical stories of justice?

3. What strategies were used and developed in these stories? By individuals? By coalitions?

4. Where do you see your congregation in relation to Chapter 5 concerns and efforts for justice?

5. What risks were involved in seeking justice as compared to risks in doing nothing?

6. What did you learn about "people power" and "collective efficacy"?

7. What justice issues in our society were not addressed in Chapter 5?

8. In evaluating these justice narratives, what changes would you suggest theologically and pragmatically?

A Homiletical Postscript

Staying the Course with Micah, Jesus, and the Communion of Saints

Do not be conformed to this world, but be transformed by the renewal of your minds, so that you may discern what is the will of God.

Romans 12:2

Since we are surrounded by so great a cloud of witnesses, let us also lay aside every weight and sin that cling so closely, and let us run with perseverance the race that is set before us, looking to Jesus the pioneer and perfecter of our faith.

Hebrews 12:1-2

In Luke's gospel, Chapter 10:17-20, seventy of Jesus' followers return from a mission to heal the sick and announce the Reign of God. They are beside themselves with success, higher than a kite, filled with joy. "Lord, in your name even the demons submit to us." In effect these faithful followers are saying, "All of the training and preparation you have given us works! When can we celebrate? Then send us out again."

Surely any wise leader would reinforce his followers' success with congratulations, a news release in the Jerusalem Times, a trophy ceremony, and announcement of the disciple of the month. Apparently Jesus has no motivational training. He offers a cryptic response confirming their authority, yet concludes, "nevertheless, do not rejoice at this, that the spirits submit to you, but rejoice that your names are written in heaven."

Do not rejoice? Talk about air coming out of your balloon. About raining on your parade. While not reported in the text, we can easily imagine the disciples' response. Silence. Disbelief. Bewilderment. Even anger. And unstated thoughts and feelings: "Lord, we've done what you sent us to do. Now you throw a wet blanket on our success in your name. Give us a break!"

So what's going on here? Is Jesus opposed to success? Surely he is not encouraging resignation or passivity. After all he is the one who sent them out to be advocates and agents for God's Reign. Is he saying your success is all well and good, but what really counts is not earthly good works but your future in heaven? Or just the opposite, namely, that your good works are your ticket to heaven?

I believe this passage in Luke is both dangerous and deliverance-filled. It's brimming with vulnerable edges, almost begging to be misunderstood. On the other hand, it's a safeguard for staying the course with our vocation of justice.

Jesus seems to direct attention away from momentary success, a caution about getting hooked on results, even good results. If our deepest rejoicing is experienced when things work out favorably, who are we when desired outcome is absent, even seemingly crushed. Who are we when the demons of injustice and violence are not subject to our best efforts? Victorious athletes, among others, sometimes give God credit for their success. Give me an athlete on the losing side who thanks God in spite of loss and I'll show you a person likely of genuine faith.

Of course we feel good, blessed, and excited when attendance at church is up, when new members come aboard, when pledges to the budget and to special mission causes are better than last year, when we see love and hospitality taking place within and beyond the congregation. Of course it's special when our vocation of justice produces fruitful results benefiting those in special need. Of course we are joyful when faith and politics come together for the common good.

Jesus' words "rejoice that your names are written in heaven" may have alluded to the idea in the Hebrew bible of a heavenly book of life with names of the righteous. The rejoicing recommended by Jesus has to do with being included in God's covenant and work in the world. Jesus wants our most profound rejoicing to be deeper than momentary success or feel-good experiences. Maybe the book of life reference is akin to the Righteous Among the Nations" at Yad Vashem, Israel's national Holocaust Memorial in Jerusalem. The Memorial commemorates the role of non-Jews who tried to save Jews from the Nazis. More than 13,000 names are inscribed on the righteous wall of honor. Instead of a book of life, a wall of life.

We are empowered to stay the course, not because the percentages are usually on our side, but because God keeps calling us to be God's people of love, peace, and justice. Rejoice that your life is embraced in the life of God and that you are forever part of God's dream for God's creation.

Dean Brackley, S.J., a faculty member at the University of Central America in San Salvador, reinforces God's gift of sustaining power: "It is central to our dignity that each of us human beings has a vocation. A vocation is not something we just up and decide on, like picking out a shirt in a store. It is something we discover. My vocation might be to raise children, discover new planets, drive a truck, lead a social movement, or a combination of these. But more than something to do, a vocation is who I am, or might become. For most people music is a pleasant pastime or a hobby, but for some, like Pablo Casals, it is destiny: the way of life that unlocks their most creative energies. When we discover our vocation, something clicks inside. We feel we have found what we were born for. Discovering my vocation gives my life meaning and purpose. People are starved for that today. Although vocations vary greatly, we all share a deepest vocation as human beings: the vocation to love and serve."[1]

The Communion of Saints

My friend Zan Holmes speaks of "stacking the gallery" as part of his preaching preparation. He imagines a gathering of significant others who call for his best effort and who stand near as a supportive cast. I find his idea helpful as also applied to the Christian vocation of justice. Living persons who are exemplars of justice come to mind offering both challenge and hope. I also recall those now of blessed memory who spoke out and lived justice. Some I knew in person. Others like

Martin Luther King, Jr., Abraham Joshua Heschel, and Oscar Romero remain alive through writings, homilies, and books about them. They serve as mentors and keep us humble and hopeful.

There was a time when the church's notion or doctrine of "the communion of saints" had very little meaning to me. The term inevitably brings forth different images and understandings. For some it seems to point to an amorphous aggregate of previous faith travelers "up there or out there" somewhere. For others a very definite sense of those to whom we are indebted comes to mind aided by hymns of gratitude and remembrance. For me the communion of saints has become a very present reality. While death does end a life as we have known it here and now, death does not end the meaning of a life. As often said, we stand on the shoulders of significant others who have gone before us. They continue to be our mentors, nurturing us when we become discouraged and keeping our feet on the ground when we are tempted to think more highly of ourselves than we ought to think. Who are your "communion of justice saints?" Stack your gallery and let them give you strength and guidance as you seek to do justice, love mercy, and walk humbly with God.

A Franciscan Benediction

May God bless us with discomfort …
At easy answers, half truths,
And superficial relationships,
So that we may live deep within our hearts.

May God bless us with anger …
At injustice, oppression, and
Exploitation of people,
So that we may work
For justice, freedom, and peace.

May God bless us with tears …
To shed for those who suffer from
Pain, rejection, starvation, and war.
So that we may reach out our hands

To comfort them
And to turn their pain into JOY.

And may God bless us with enough
Foolishness ...
To believe that
We can make a difference in this world,
So that we can DO
What others claim cannot be done.
Amen.

Notes

[1]Dean Brackley, S. J., *Higher Standards for Higher Education: The Christian University and Solidarity*, address presented at Universidad de Centroamerica, San Salvador, El Salvador, March, 2003.

APPENDIX A

An Inevitable Connection: Peace and Justice

The saying "if you want peace, work for justice" is well known by most Christians of whatever theological position. The two are so closely connected that the title of the book, with some shift of emphasis, could have been *Becoming a Peacemaking Congregation*. Yet because this book focuses more on justice, I wanted to name their interdependence here.

There can be no genuine peace or reconciliation apart from justice. Nobel Laureate Muhammad Yunus expresses the connection between peace and justice: "Peace should be understood in a human way – in a broad social, political, and economic way. Peace is threatened by unjust economic, social, and political order, absence of democracy, environmental degradation and absence of human rights."[1]

The 8th to 6th centuries B.C.E. Hebrew prophets insist that the pre-condition for peace is the coming together of truth and justice. Jesus unites peace and justice in the Beatitudes: "Blessed are those who hunger and thirst for righteousness … blessed are the peacemakers." Notice how the Beatitudes also embrace Micah's trilogy of God's requirement: "Blessed are the poor in spirit" echoes walking humbly with God, and "Blessed are the merciful" reflects Micah's "love mercy."

Just as peace in the deepest sense is dependent on justice, it also is true that justice is more likely under conditions of peace. Listen to the late Rabbi Abraham Heschel: "When the prophets appeared, they proclaimed that might is not supreme, that the sword is an abomination, that violence is obscene. The sword, they said, shall be destroyed:

'They shall beat their swords into plowshares
And their spears into pruning hooks;

Nation shall not lift up sword against nation,
Neither shall they learn war any more.'
... Isaiah 2:4 and Micah 4:3"[2]

"The prophets, questioning man's infatuation with might, insisted not only on the immorality but also the futility and absurdity of war."[3]

"Righteousness and peace are interdependent (Ps. 85:10). The condemnation of violence is a major theme in the prophets' speeches."[4]

Many Christians seem to have forgotten that the One to whom we profess loyalty is the Prince of Peace who blessed the peacemakers. Peacemaking, working hand in hand with justice, constitutes what should be the Magnificent Obsession for Christians. How do we better love the world in the name of the God of Peace than being faithful to peace and justice? How do we better follow Jesus than to insist that the world's future must develop nonviolent alternatives to bloated military budgets, expanding empire, and preemptive war which is itself a form of terror.

Commitment to nonviolence suggests a culture of life rather than a culture of death. A life oriented culture increases human capital for social resources on behalf of the common good. Education, health care, and quality of life have a better chance of thriving when the prophets' vision of peace is honored. One cannot assume that resources not spent on war will automatically find their way to life improving ends. Yet a mindset dedicated to peace rather than war is more likely to develop public policy enhancing "the beloved community" about which Martin Luther King, Jr., spoke. A climate of peace building makes a people more aware of injustice to be addressed.

In Chapter 5 there is a story in which a United Methodist congregation and Muslims from two mosques reversed the biases of each group and discovered a transformative sense of community and acceptance of each other. The United Methodist pastor came to see the shared events as a process of peacemaking. He surmised that if the new Muslim friends were unjustly treated by their neighbors, the press, or the U.S. government, their United Methodist friends would more likely stand up and be advocates for justice. So while justice is the pre-condition of peace, commitment to peaceful and hospitable relationships can overcome prejudice and contribute to advocacy for a more humane and just society.

NOTES

[1]Muhammad Yunus, The Progressive Christian, November/December, 2007.
[2]Abraham Heschel, *The Prophets*, 1962, p. 203.
[3]Heschel, pp 203-204.
[4]Heschel, p. 206

APPENDIX B

A Less Recognized Connection: Pastoral and Prophetic Ministry

It took me many years in ordained ministry to realize the mutuality and interdependence of pastoral ministry with the vocation of justice. My failure to see this connection was due to a bad case of theological myopia. I saw these ministries from my own limited perspective instead of from God's viewpoint. One reason to pay attention to the Hebrew prophets is that they can teach us to approach life and ministry from the much broader view of Divine purpose.

While we may visualize pastoral ministry as comforting the afflicted and prophetic vocation as afflicting the comfortable, these are half-truths blind to God's dream for the earth, namely, wellbeing or shalom for all. Pastoral ministry, while a responsibility of the whole congregation, tends to relate to individuals or small groups whereas prophetic ministry frequently connects with systems or large groups of people. Said in another way, pastoral ministry is ordinarily based on personal relationships while prophetic outreach is often about group action and public policy.

Worth remembering is the fact that insightful pastoral counseling, a function of pastoral ministry, does not necessarily lead to a smooth or comfortable outcome. On the other hand, the history of progressive public policy as the face of prophetic vocation has brought great comfort and broader human rights to multitudes of those previously disadvantaged in our society. In American history Christian evangelicals and progressives have contributed to labor rights, women's suffrage, and equality under law for minorities.

Souls and systems inevitably interact with each other for either wellbeing or deformity of life. Martin Luther said the law (the system) becomes a silent teacher. This tacit "curriculum" of the way reality is ordered in a given society becomes internalized by both those harmed by it and those who seemingly benefit. Martin Luther King, Jr., captured the sense of individual and systemic interdependence: "We are caught in an inescapable network of mutuality, tied together in a single garment of destiny."[1]

When pastors and laity see the pastoral and the prophetic as a seamless garment of God's dream for all humankind instead of in conflict with each other, the church's ministry takes on a unity and wholeness of purpose not otherwise experienced.

Notes

[1]Martin Luther King, Jr., "The Man Who Was a Fool," in *Strength to Love*, Fortress Press, 1963, p. 70.